The

Spiritual

Road

to

Self-Esteem

The

Spiritual

Road

to

Self-Esteem

————————

KIM MICHAELS

MORE TO LIFE PUBLISHING

www.morepublish.com

E-mail: info@morepublish.com

For foreign and translation rights, contact Nigel J. Yorwerth.

E-mail: nigel@PublishingCoaches.com

Cover design: Nita Ybarra

ISBN: 978-0-9825746-5-2

10 9 8 7 6 5 4 3 2 1

The names and some details of the stories used throughout this book have been changed to protect the privacy of those who have shared their lessons on lifes's path. The information and insights in this book are solely the opinion of the author and should not be considered as a form of therapy, advice, direction, diagnosis, and/or treatment of any kind. This information is not a substitute for medical, psychological, or other professional advice, counseling and care. All matters pertaining to your individual health should be supervised by a physician or appropriate health-care practitioner. No guarantee is made by the author or the publisher that the practices described in this book will yield successful results for anyone at any time. They are presented for informational purposes only, as the practice and proof rests with the individual.

CONTENTS

PROLOGUE

I wrote this book because those of us who are spiritual seekers face a double challenge when it comes to developing self-esteem. One aspect of our predicament is that many of us have been ostracized or persecuted because of our beliefs. As a result we start out with a self-esteem deficit that is larger than many of the people around us have. The other challenge we face is that we do not seek self-esteem the way most people in our materialistic culture do. We don't buy into the idea that our worth depends on the size of our cars, houses, body parts or bank accounts. Consequently, we need to find a spiritual approach to self-esteem and that is precisely what this book will describe.

I will outline a systematic, gradual path that anyone can follow. This path will take you through the seven steps or stages that most of us follow on the spiritual path. By understanding these stages you will be able to work through your current stage more quickly and make faster progress towards a deeper, more genuine form of self-esteem.

I hope this book will help you attain what I see as the driving force behind spiritual growth, namely "breakthrough experiences." What is a breakthrough experience? We live in a society and time when rational, analytical, linear thinking is considered the answer to all of our problems. A breakthrough experience is completely beyond the rational, intellectual and linear mind.

Over many years, I have observed thousands of people who attempted to deal with spirituality and spiritual growth by using the intellectual mind. We also have the ability to step outside the rational mind and have an experience that is completely nonlinear and simply cannot be dealt with analytically. I am not hereby saying that the rational mind is an enemy of spiritual growth. The rational mind is a very necessary tool, both for practical living and for spiritual pursuits. The rational mind can indeed help us increase our understanding of spiritual concepts. This can, if used correctly, set a foundation for what really helps us move forward, namely breakthrough experiences. Such breakthroughs can happen only if we do not get trapped in the analytical mind, wanting to force everything into the kind of mental boxes used by this mind. In order to make full use of a tool, you also have to know the limitations of the tool so you know when to put it down and reach for another tool.

This is also true for the analytical mind. Trying to attain self-esteem exclusively through the intellect will inevitably put you in a blind alley. The simple reason is that the intellect can argue for and against anything. If you constantly have to defend your sense of self-esteem, then you do not have true self-esteem. You will never get beyond the dilemma of the intellect unless you acknowledge that there are some things in life and on the spiritual path that simply cannot be grasped by the analytical mind. If you want to experience these nonlinear phenomena, you must stop analyzing and open your mind to a direct experience, namely what the ancients called "gnosis." The concept means oneness between the knower and the known.

A breakthrough experience is when you step outside of, silence or neutralize the rational mind. It is when you have a sense of being connected to a greater mind outside your own self, something that you cannot define but that nevertheless feels completely real. You feel like a new perspective, even a new world, has opened up to you. You feel like you are seeing things the way they are for the first time. You recognize a truth that you know is real, even though you cannot explain why in a rational, linear way—you just know that you know it. You feel like your life or consciousness is shifting and you know certain things will never be the same. You know you have touched the sublime and that you are flowing with the ever-transcending stream we call life.

1 | *The* **TRUE SOURCE** *of* **SELF-ESTEEM**

Take a look at the word *self-esteem*. It has two parts, and in my experience most people look at the word like this:

self-ESTEEM

They focus on the result they want to achieve, namely that they want to feel they are good enough, they want to feel they have worth and that their lives have a purpose. They seem to think that esteem is produced outside the self and then directed at the self. The effect is that their minds focus on attaining outer conditions that will supposedly give them self-esteem. In this book, I propose a different approach. I propose we look at the word this way:

SELF-esteem

In reality, self-esteem is an inner condition—it is something that happens inside of us. Why would a specific outer condition be the only or the most effective way to produce an inner condition? Why not start by dealing with the mind directly, seeking to find out what the self really is? How can we find esteem for the self if we do not know what the self is? What if true self-esteem is produced inside the self—if it is the self esteeming itself?

In this book, I describe a viable, systematic path that will take you to true and lasting self-esteem by helping you get to know the self—your *true* self. This path can work for anyone, but it is not a quick-fix and it will take time and require effort. The results you get will be lasting because they will not depend on outer conditions. Nobody in this world can take your self-esteem away from you for the simple reason that nobody gave it to you. It comes from inside the self and it is self-sustainable.

It has been my experience that the only road to self-esteem is to know the self, and the only way to know the self is to take a spiritual approach. What do I mean when I say "spiritual"? I mean something that is universal and open-ended. A spiritual outlook means we accept that there is a level of reality beyond the material world. We cannot detect the spiritual realm with our senses, but we can know something about it and we can even experience it directly through the intuitive abilities of the mind. At the same time, our knowledge of this spiritual realm cannot be confined to one particular religion or philosophy or a set of doctrines and dogmas that are set in stone.

The essence of the spiritual path is that we can raise our consciousness to a higher level. Once we are at that level, we will understand and experience things we simply cannot grasp at our current level of consciousness. From that new place of awareness, we are able to raise our consciousness to an even higher level, and this process will not stop as long as we are on earth. The path is an ongoing process that will lead us to progressively higher levels of consciousness. At our present level, we simply cannot grasp where the path will end or if it ever does. Thus, the opportunity before us right now is to focus on transcending our current level and reaching the next level up.

While the process is ongoing, there are distinct levels. Once you get to a certain stage, you will begin to feel a deeper appreciation for who you are and why you are here on earth. You will also get a strong sense that life has a general purpose and that your life has a specific purpose. This will give you a sense of self-esteem that is far beyond anything you can get through outer means. Only the self can truly esteem itself, but it can do so only when it knows itself.

Solid and shaky self-esteem

To understand what real self-esteem is, we need to explore the difference between two forms of self-esteem: solid and shaky. I define shaky self-esteem as a form of esteem that depends on factors outside yourself, such as your status in society, what you own or other people's opinions. This form of esteem is not likely to last because it depends on factors that can be difficult or impossible for you to control. If external factors change, then the way you look at yourself must also change.

I still remember when, during a spiritual conference, I was given a ride by Stephen, a young man who had grown up in one of Boston's better families, had received a Corvette for his sixteenth birthday and had graduated from an Ivy League college. During the 20-minute ride, he talked almost nonstop and he only talked about himself, his family, what they owned and how he was destined for a career in politics, possibly becoming a senator. In reflecting on the experience, I couldn't understand why Stephen had such a need to impress a total stranger he might never meet again. The only explanation I could see was that his behavior reflected his inner insecurities. In Stephen's mind his self-esteem was tied up in outer things, such as his family background, his education and his wealth. I was a stranger, so I knew nothing of Stephen's background and therefore I gave him no special status. That was unbearable to Stephen, so without realizing it, he proceeded to educate me so that I could give him the proper status. The more I seemed unimpressed, the more he wanted to impress me and he seemed very uncomfortable at the end of the ride.

In contrast, solid self-esteem depends on nothing outside the self. According to just about every spiritual tradition, we all have the potential to take control over what is happening inside the sphere of the self. In fact, I believe this self-mastery is the real goal of our spiritual quest. Once we attain this mastery over self, we attain a form of esteem that will not change with the whims of external factors. It will be based on something that will last because it is based on who we are, not what we do or what we own. Attaining solid self-esteem is not difficult because it is actually the natural state of the self. Both the lack of self-esteem and shaky self-esteem are unnatural conditions, and that is why it is a never-ending struggle to attain and maintain shaky self-esteem.

Look at how many people in our modern world struggle to create the outer conditions that will supposedly produce self-esteem. How do most people seek the feeling of esteem for themselves? By living up to some outer criteria, some outer standard. This may give people a sense of self-esteem as long as they live up to the standard, but what if you never lived up to the prevailing standard in your environment or what if you no longer live up to the standard? One obvious standard is beauty. How many young girls have been scarred for life because they did not live up to the standard of beauty projected by the advertising industry in order to sell more products? How many women have spent a significant part of their lives seeking to buy compliance with this standard? Yet no matter how much money you have, can you buy youthful beauty forever? What happens when time runs out and you no longer live up to the standard? The self-esteem you had built based on outer criteria collapses and what is left?

Another standard is your job, career or position in society. How many young boys have been scarred for life because their fathers did not have the most prestigious jobs? How many men have spent a significant part of their lives seeking to attain a better job or a higher income in order to prove their worth? In the book *The End of Suffering,* Russel Targ describes how he used to work for Lockheed, and there was a real sense that Lockheed engineers were part of something special. Yet he noticed that once those engineers retired, most of them were dead within two years. They simply couldn't handle no longer being part of something special. Apparently being part of the human race was not special enough.

I personally experienced this in my family. My entire family came from working-class roots and I was the first person to get a high-school diploma. My father turned 18 just as the second world war started and my native Denmark was occupied by Nazi Germany. That made the already scarce jobs even scarcer and he spent the rest of his life working in factories. His older brother did better and worked his way up in the telephone company until he became the manager of his district. We were all proud of his achievements, but two years after his retirement we attended his funeral. Speaking of Denmark, international studies have established that Denmark is the country in which people are the happiest. Even Oprah Winfrey did a show about the happy people in Denmark. At the same time, a growing number of people there receive psychological treatment for depression or more severe mental illnesses. In 2012 a national association in the health field predicted that over the coming decades mental illness will become the greatest national health challenge. If the happiest people in the world have such problems, when will the trend spread to the United States? Given that I have lived in the U.S. for 22 years, I know many people who say it has already arrived.

How can we explain this? Why don't people automatically become happy or content as material affluence grows? Even though people have a comfortable and secure material lifestyle, why don't they attain a lasting sense of self-esteem? What is missing? To me, the explanation is that we simply do not know enough about the self—we do not know who, or what, we are.

Why don't we already have self-esteem?

Let's take this one step further. Think about a person you really admire. You have esteem for this person but you are not that person. You are esteeming that person from a distance. You are a self who is esteeming a separate self, and that is not self-esteem. In fact, no matter how much you admire the other person, it is possible that he or she still has low self-esteem. One of the most severe consequences of low self-esteem is when people contemplate or actually commit suicide. I once knew a young man who was severely depressed and one day attempted suicide. All of his friends were surprised because they admired him for his positive qualities. Even though many of them had tried to help him out of his depression, he had not actually heard what they were trying to tell him. Having other people esteem you is no guarantee that you can esteem yourself.

When you admire another person, you are a self who is esteeming the self of the other person. Yet the other self may not share your esteem. In fact, the two selves may have opposite views. Now transfer this to how you look at yourself. What does it actually mean that you have esteem for yourself? Is the "you" that has the feeling of esteem different from the "self" that is being esteemed?

This is no mere play on words because there is a profound truth hidden here, as we will explore later. For now, I want to point out that the main reason our modern society cannot give us true and lasting self-esteem is that it cannot provide us with a meaningful understanding of what the self is.

We can now see that if we are to find a deeper and more lasting sense of self-esteem than we get from outer standards, we have to increase our understanding of the self. We have to engage in a quest to discover what the self is; we have to walk the road of self-discovery. I believe that road must be a spiritual road.

Why does our modern society fail to give most of us genuine self-esteem? I still remember one day in elementary school when our history teacher told us how people in medieval times believed the earth was flat. He turned it into a good joke and the entire class laughed, including me. Afterwards, I had the thought: "But what will people who live 500 years from now say about our time?" We tend to think that our Western civilization is the most advanced ever, but many of the civilizations of the past also thought of themselves that way. We look back at the people who thought the earth was flat and wonder how anyone could believe in such a silly idea. Yet will coming generations think some our most cherished beliefs about life are equally primitive?

I think they will, and I think there is one area they will find especially primitive. They will see that we had quite sophisticated technology (although primitive compared to their own), but they will wonder how a civilization that could send men to the moon could fail to teach its own children how to find genuine self-esteem and happiness. They will wonder how our civilization could fail to give its children a method for understanding and mastering their own minds. After all, the psyche is the one thing that affects everything we do in life.

I think future civilizations will have acknowledged the simple truth that we are psycho-spiritual beings. This will make them see our time as primitive because right now we don't actually have a clear definition of what kind of beings we are. Are we created by a remote God or are we evolved apes? Do we live in a world guided by God's laws or by mere chance? Did a God, who is supposedly good and just, create us as sinners or are we the products of random events? Mainstream Christianity and scientific materialism are the two main paradigms or thought systems that dominate our society, and if either of them had given you self-esteem, why would you be reading this book?

I have met many people on the spiritual path who grew up in a Christian environment. Some have been able to sincerely apply Christian principles and thereby build a sense of self-esteem. Many others were so affected by the claim that they are sinners and that Jesus was so special compared to them that they never built a healthy sense of self-esteem. Interestingly, one of Jesus' most enigmatic statements says: "The kingdom of God is within you." What is within you but the self? How will you ever enter that kingdom unless you know the self? Perhaps self-knowledge and the raising of consciousness are the true keys to grasping and applying the inner teachings of Jesus. Perhaps only those who know the self can find the strait and narrow way of Christ.

Whether you consider yourself a Christian, a spiritual seeker or a New Age person, how could you lose by getting to know your self better? After all, you do have to live with this self 24 hours a day, 365 days a year.

Me-esteem and we-esteem

Let's look at our situation as we grow up in modern society. Most of us have been exposed to the Christian doctrine of original sin, which says we are sinners by our very nature—even that we were created in sin. Most of us were also affected by the claim of scientific materialism, namely that we are simply animals and that our sense of self is the product of our genes or mechanical processes in the brain. How will either of those thought systems give us a foundation for solid self-esteem?

I am not trying to say we can blame all of our psychological issues on Christianity or materialism. I actually think the idea of original sin is simply one expression of a deeper underlying state of consciousness. In my extensive readings on psychology and self-help, I have noticed that a growing number of experts are beginning to talk about a collective consciousness. This started with Carl Jung, who talked about the "collective unconscious," but many others have developed similar ideas. The concept is that a group of people—even humanity as a whole—develop a collective state of consciousness that affects all people who are part of the group.

I like to look at this as a group being or entity that is constantly broadcasting certain messages into our minds. Most of us are not aware of these messages, but part of spiritual growth is to become more aware of how we are being affected by these external pressures. One of the most powerful messages projected into our minds is that we are not good enough as we are, that there is something fundamentally wrong with us and that we need to do something to make up for it. This archetypal idea is behind both the concept of original sin and the idea that we humans are nothing more than evolved apes. Both Christianity and materialism deny that we have inherent value, that the self is worthy in and of itself.

The effect of this idea is that we need to do something in order to compensate for our flaws, which involves two elements. First, there is a standard that we need to live up to and then there is a set of rules that we need to follow. In other words, our lives are simply one big game of catch-up where we are constantly seeking to run away from our inherent imperfections by living up to an external standard that promises us we will one day be delivered by reaching some perfect state. Each society has its own standards for how you can be delivered. I have already mentioned physical beauty, position in society and money, but there are many others.

The result is that you really have only two ways to go. One is that you can pick a standard and attempt to become so good at a certain task that you stand out from the crowd and become someone special. You attain esteem by standing out as an individual. I would like to call this "me-esteem."

The other option is that you can melt into a certain group so you don't attract any attention by being different. You attain esteem by not standing out as an individual but by conforming to a group. I would like to call this "we-esteem."

In my observation, neither me-esteem nor we-esteem will last forever, nor will they give you genuine self-esteem. The reason is simple: They don't come from inside the self but are dependent upon outer factors.

This inevitably puts you in conflict or competition with other people for the simple reason that you build esteem only by comparing yourself to others. This makes it very tempting to engage in the twofold action of both seeking to raise yourself up and put others down. The price you pay is that you are now trapped in a never-ending competition with others. You are defining yourself in relation to others.

One example of this is what is called a social pecking order whereby the population is divided into layers, each with a different status. If you seem too different from the members of a certain group, they will feel threatened by you and they will turn you into a scapegoat. By putting you down as being in a lower category, they can build up their own illusion of because at least they are better than somebody. Most people in modern society have found some group to which they belong and they have accepted the we-esteem that this gives them.

Why spiritual people have low self-esteem

The trouble with most spiritual people is that we simply don't fit into the established groups in society. Over the past 36 years I have known hundreds of people who became spiritual seekers precisely because it wasn't enough for them to live normal lives. One example is George, who said: "My parent's were solid middle class people, and they wanted the best for me, but they thought that meant I would have more of what they had. I just never locked in to the American dream. I couldn't see working the same job for 40 years and competing with the neighbors on building on to the house, getting bigger cars, bigger riding lawnmowers and a bigger swimming pool as the goal of life. I didn't want more of what my parents had; I wanted more than they had. I wanted something more meaningful than what they had. It just wasn't enough for me to live that way."

Those of us who accept that life has a spiritual side have the potential to go beyond both me-esteem and we-esteem. We have the potential to help society move beyond this eternal struggle between competing groups. The reason is that as spiritual seekers we don't fit into any of the groups in the social pecking order. We are often looked down upon by three groups of people. Christians accuse us of being of the devil. Materialists accuse us of being superstitious fools. And people who are indifferent to both Christianity and materialism think we are too far "out there," wherever that might be. I discovered the spiritual path when I was 18 and I joined a movement that promoted a form of Eastern meditation. I quickly learned that people felt threatened by my interest in spirituality. There was not a single person in my family with religious or spiritual interests and they reacted as if I had committed some kind of treason. I really don't know what could have been worse in the eyes of my family members than joining a spiritual group "that was just out to get my money."

They reacted as if I had done the most stupid thing they could possibly imagine, and they made this abundantly clear to me at a particular dinner party. I remember afterwards feeling like I was suddenly all alone in the world with no family to lean on for support. I simply could no longer identify with people who reacted so negatively because I was interested in something they did not understand and did not want to understand. I had not really expected them to understand my spirituality, but I had hoped they would try to understand *me*.

Things were no better at the Danish university I attended at the time. This was back in the "good old days" before the illusions of communism came tumbling down, so there was still a large group of believing Marxists. They were extraordinarily negative towards me and a few other people who did a project related to spirituality.

In 1987 I moved to the United States in order to pursue my spiritual interests and here I often met Christians who were very negative towards my "New Age" beliefs. I still remember how Will, a very kind builder, invited me to his home in an attempt to "save me." I really liked Will and had no desire whatsoever to hurt his feelings. I also had to admit that he had not thought as deeply about spiritual topics as I had and thus he had little chance of converting me to his fundamentalist beliefs. It was a delicate balance to reject his conversion attempt without making him feel rejected. I don't think I succeeded because he never talked to me again. I even experienced how a particular spiritual group became the target of an incredible campaign by government agencies, politicians, local people and the press. I believe such deliberate and systematic persecution would have created a public outcry in a small country like Denmark, but in the "land of the free and the home of the brave," no one blinked an eye. It was, quite frankly, a major shock to experience how impersonal things can be in a country as big as the United States. I have never felt more alone and powerless than I sometimes felt when dealing with representatives of the American government. At the same time I have never met more kind and genuinely selfless people than in the United States. One wonders why the consciousness of the people isn't reflected in the government.

I have met many spiritual people who likewise felt like outcasts. For example, several American friends grew up in Catholic families and they have all told me how the local priest had no answers to their spiritual questions and managed to make them feel bad for asking them. The result of such experiences is that we often start the spiritual path with a self-esteem deficit.

We feel low self-esteem from growing up in modern society, but on top of that we feel low self-esteem because we are spiritual and so different. The problem with this is that it can set our spiritual path on a nonconstructive track from the very beginning, because we now seek to use the path as a way to compensate for our lack of self-esteem. We take the deficit approach to the spiritual path and to our quest for self-esteem.

Let me revisit the negative reaction I got from my family when I joined my first spiritual movement. Today I can see that their reaction was in part due to the fact that they could see that I was taking an unbalanced approach. The adults clearly saw that in my youthful optimism I was being naive in thinking my spiritual movement had the solution to all of the world's problems.

What my family members did not see was that this naiveté was due to the fact that I had grown up in a society with no spiritual tradition. I had been brought up to be a good consumer of everything from toothpaste to houses, but I had no knowledge whatsoever of how to be a good consumer in the spiritual marketplace. My only way to become a better consumer was to sample what was available and learn through experience.

The quest for superiority

What I have learned over the past 36 years is that most spiritual people have to go through a period of experimentation. We simply have to get some feel for the spiritual path and the various movements, philosophies or gurus available. In the process of learning, it is both unavoidable and necessary that we sometimes make mistakes or go too far into one extreme or another. Yet why should we all have to make the same mistakes? Why should we all have to reinvent the wheel? In the rest of this chapter, I will describe some examples of how the deficit approach can derail our spiritual quest, causing us to seek me-esteem and we-esteem in ways that can never provide self-esteem.

I was never a conformist, yet neither was I a competitor. I never enjoyed sports and in school I never tried to get better grades than others. However, I was a person who liked to do the unusual, even the extreme. I like to feel that I have done as much as I possibly can, but I also see that sometimes I become unbalanced in my drive to do as much as possible. When I found the spiritual path I had no problem giving up the comfortable materialistic lifestyle I was brought up to pursue. I had just graduated as an architect when I left Denmark, knowing I could not use my degree in the United States. For the past 25 years my life has revolved around my spiritual growth, which has caused me at times to live my life in a way that I now see as unbalanced. In retrospect, I can see that much of it was aimed at producing a sense of me-esteem by using spiritual activities to make myself seem special, even superior. I have met many people who did the same thing, and I would like to describe some of the ways I have seen people use the spiritual path to build a sense of being special or superior.

When you pursue self-esteem by being superior, the dynamic is simple. The more you stand out from the crowd, the more esteem you have. The need for being special can combine with the sense that as a spiritual person you have been ostracized and ignored by family and friends. You could compensate for that if it suddenly turned out that you were actually superior from the very beginning. What could make you superior? There is an entire industry out there that is aimed at making spiritual people feel special—all in return for a fee.

One example of this is astrology. Now, I am not saying astrology is useless, but I have seen countless spiritual seekers enter the race to find some trine or square in the umpteenth house, showing that they were born with psychic abilities or the potential to bring balance to the intergalactic alignment. I never saw people develop lasting self-esteem this way. Another avenue is psychics who come in all shapes and sizes. I found the spiritual path before the advent of the internet, but now you can find a dizzying array of psychics. When I was in the mediation movement, quite a few people had received drawings of their auras. You sent cash and a photo to an address in England, and an old man would use his clairvoyant abilities to draw a picture of your personal aura. A friend showed me hers, and it was a circle with some colored fields and figures, almost like an abstract painting. You could pretty much read anything into it you wanted.

There was a Danish psychic who had half of the members of the meditation movement as her clients. I never felt any prompting to go to her, so I don't know exactly what she did. I simply observed that she had a talent for giving people a sense of being special, but not so special that they didn't need to come back for another session. I knew adults who simply would not make a decision without first getting a reading from this lady. Even though I was young at the time, I clearly saw that this was not the way I wanted to live my life. I have always felt that it is my responsibility to make my own decisions and I have never liked it when anyone has tried to influence my decision-making process.

Today you can go on the internet and book a telephone or online consultation with just about any kind of psychic you can imagine. Especially noteworthy to me is the concept that you can schedule a session where an ascended master or intergalactic being will give you a personal reading or dictation through the psychic.

I find it hard to believe that a genuine spiritual master will tell me what to do when such a master should know that I will grow only by making my own decisions. For some people I have met, having a cosmic being give them personal instructions gives them a clear sense of being validated by the highest authority. One example was Ed, who used to get readings from a cosmic master through a psychic and then insisted on calling me afterwards to tell me all about it, even to the point of mimicking the voice used by this being. I have known people who were told that they would personally play a crucial role in the cosmic plan for saving the earth, and this gave them a strong feeling of me-esteem. Personally I feel that when you have self-esteem, you realize that none of us are more special than others because we all have a part to play in the cosmic plan. In fact, we *are* the cosmic plan.

The quest for psychic abilities

Just as there are people who love to go to psychics, there are people who have a desire to have or develop psychic abilities. For example, Jody was constantly dreaming about opening her third eye so she could see people's auras. She imagined that once her third eye was open, she would instantly become famous and have people come to her for advice. In her eyes, that was the highest form of me-esteem.

I have met a few people who had psychic abilities. Eli, for example, could see people's auras and would sometimes get premonitions about future events in their lives. You could also show him a deck of playing cards one at a time and afterwards he could tell you the exact order of the cards. Eli rarely made other people aware of his abilities and he didn't try to make money on it. There is a fundamental difference between seeking to help people on a more spontaneous basis and then setting up appointments and charging people money.

I have always been fascinated by science and according to some physicists, Einstein's famous equation, $E=mc^2$ means that we live in a world where everything is energy. Different forms of energy are set apart by vibration so there are several levels of vibration, including the material world and a number of levels in the spiritual realm.

There is a level of vibration above and beyond the material world, and this is where you find true spiritual masters. I do believe it is possible for us to communicate with beings in a higher realm and that many people are meant to do so in this age. It is also clear to me that there are levels of vibration that are beyond the material world but lower than the spiritual realm. In these lower realms you find all kinds of beings who are willing to give you validation—if you are willing to give them your soul.

A true spiritual master has ascended to a higher realm than earth. This means that such a master needs nothing from you, neither energy nor anything else. In contrast, a being in a lower realm has not ascended and thus it does need to get energy and attention from you. If you agree to give energy to these beings, they may give you a sense of being superior. But in the long run I don't see this doing anything for your spiritual growth. I have seen some rather scary examples of how this has caused people to go to such extremes that they could not pull themselves back into balance.

For example, Georgine felt she had been told by spiritual beings that she was the incarnation of a goddess. This gave her a sense of me-esteem for several years, but then it simply wasn't enough for her. She was then told by her spirit guides that she was a twin soul of a cosmic being. After some time, she was told that she was also the twin flame of other ascended beings. But where will she go next? How much higher can you go in this game of seeking ultimate validation through external status? And when will she instead go within, find her true self and realize that it is perfectly enough to be just one spiritual being among all the others? After all, we are all one so the only way to raise yourself is to raise the whole.

Courses that make you feel superior

There is an entire industry aimed at offering you classes or courses that supposedly give you spiritual or psychic abilities or raise your consciousness to a supranormal level. In the meditation movement, I knew a man named John who took a six-month residential course in Switzerland. He practiced advanced meditation techniques that no one else knew about. When he came home from this very expensive course, he had the title "Governor of the Age of Enlightenment." The implications were clear: He had raised his consciousness to such a superhuman level that he had the powers of mind to actually direct society into a new and better age. Unfortunately, John also acted as if he was above and beyond anyone else and this quickly alienated his old friends and his fiancée.

You can find a lot of offerings on the internet that will make all kinds of lofty promises. This can be anything from initiations into secret societies to being anointed by intergalactic beings. It can also be courses aimed at developing your abilities to serve as a healer. Mary, for example, took class after class, often at great inconvenience and expense, always hoping that the next class would be the one to give her the abilities she desired. She thought that if only she could heal other people, she would become someone special.

I don't think taking a class is necessarily worthless. But I have learned to evaluate whether a class is aimed at helping you transcend your present sense of self or validating that sense of self. I have also noticed that if you seek special abilities out of a desire to boost your me-esteem, those abilities will often allude you. Spiritual abilities are a gift not given to those who desire them with impure motives.

Using divination to appear superior

Some courses offer to teach you how to use a form of divination. Divination is the use of a mechanical technique or device for getting answers to specific questions. In the old days, a

Roman emperor going into battle would call in an oracle who would kill a pigeon, cut it open and then divine from the shape of its entrails whether the emperor would win or lose. Other examples are Ouija boards, crystal balls, Tarot cards, coffee grinds, tea leaves and an array of different techniques.

For example, muscle testing is based on using the muscle reflexes of the body for getting answers to yes-or-no questions. If your muscle is weak, the answer is no, and if it is strong, the answer is yes. Sheila learned muscle testing during a course on Health Kinesiology, which was designed to help people identify and resolve emotional blocks. Sheila, against the advice of her instructors, took muscle testing as a way to get answers to all kinds of questions, such as whether to buy a certain horse or used car and even questions about cosmological matters. She simply could not make a decision about anything without muscle testing about it first. She also thought the answers were practically the word of God.

In my observation, this was largely an excuse for her unwillingness to make personal decisions. I fail to see how one can use any kind of divination as a means for contacting true masters from the spiritual realm. The reason is that I believe true masters want us to develop our ability to discern between higher and lower vibrations. In my experience, we develop this discernment only by making decisions and learning from the mistakes we inevitably make. Unfortunately, some people are so afraid of making mistakes that they want a way to know ahead of time that their decisions are always right. This is exactly what divination promises, but in my experience this attunes your mind to the lower or psychic realm. Sheila was just one example I have seen of a person who got lured by such psychic forces. Some people ended up believing they had psychic abilities and an essential role to play in saving the planet. I am not exaggerating; it can be scary to see what some people will believe in order to feel superior.

The lure of past lives

I have accepted reincarnation since I first heard about the idea, but I have no concrete knowledge of being a particular historical person in a past life. I am open to knowing if it would help me grow spiritually, but I have no strong desire to know. I have a sense that whenever it comes to playing a role in life's great theater, I have "been there, done that." Like all of us, I've experienced many different roles and I am ready to move on from this planet.

I have seen spiritual people consult psychics or use other means in order to find out who they were in a past life. If you suddenly found out that you had been an important person in a past life, you would gain instant compensation for your sense of inferiority in this life (or so it seems to the human self).

Anne told me that when she first found the spiritual path, she had met two people who lived in the same town in Denmark. They had developed a method for determining who they had been in past lives, and when Anne met them they applied the method to her as well. Anne described how she was very fascinated by this in the beginning, but then one day a small, inner voice said to her: "How likely is it that the three of us from this little town in Denmark have been incarnated as all of the famous people of history?"

On a more serious note, these two people convinced Anne that she had been Queen Victoria in a past life. When Anne studied the queen's life and saw that she was quite a tyrant, she felt very burdened by this for several years. I have seen other examples of people who supposedly identified someone's past lifetimes in an attempt to control them. I met Hans on a meditation course and he later became involved with a psychic woman who had created a small movement centered around her. She convinced Hans that in his last lifetime he had been the commandant of a Nazi concentration camp in which she had been killed. Thus, Hans owed her a karmic debt of serving her in this lifetime.

I once had a person tell me that I had been the Apostle Paul in a past life and that this proved that I was a male chauvinist for not allowing her to tell me how to run my life. A couple of weeks later, an entirely different person told me that she had received knowledge from "above" that I had been the Apostle Peter, and this proved why I would not accept her as an authority in my life. Given that Peter and Paul were living at the same time, it seems likely one of these ladies was wrong.

Or perhaps both of them were wrong because I have never been an important historical person. My conclusion is simple. It really doesn't matter who I was in a past life because what matters is not what I did but what I learned. My past lives have given me lessons and wounds that make me who I am today. My job is to heal the wounds and uncover the lessons so I can use them to raise my consciousness in this lifetime.

Uncovering some outer status I might have had in a past lifetime will not give me self-esteem because, as I have mentioned, self-esteem can come only from inside myself. Thus, instead of looking towards a past self, I need to look within and discover my real self.

Superiority in spiritual groups

My previous examples mainly relate to seeking me-esteem by being special. Joining a spiritual movement is different in that it can serve to give us me-esteem by making us feel superior and give us we-esteem by helping us blend into a group. Because many spiritual people feel like we don't fit into society, it is natural for us to seek out a group of people who share our beliefs. We often find and join one of the many spiritual groups available today.

In fact, many people I know discovered the spiritual path by coming into contact with a spiritual teacher or movement. In my experience, joining a spiritual movement can be a source of genuine spiritual growth. It is stimulating to be able to talk freely about spiritual ideas and interacting with other people can help us gain a valuable perspective on everything from our world view to our personal psychology. A spiritual teaching can also help us increase our understanding of how the world works and answer many of the questions we have had since childhood.

When it comes to self-esteem, spiritual movements can be both a help and a hindrance. For people who seek me-esteem by being superior, a spiritual movement can offer you a sense that because you are one of the few who can see the value of this particular teaching, you are one of the most advanced spiritual people on the planet. There is a general and a specific risk involved with such beliefs.

The specific risk is that you can become unbalanced and move very far into extreme beliefs. If you become superior by being different, then the more different you become, the more special you will be. There are many examples of how spiritual groups have defined a very extremist and unbalanced lifestyle as the norm for that group. Once the members have decided to accept the standard, they no longer see how unbalanced it is. For example, some religious groups will not allow members to receive blood transfusions or accept certain forms of medical treatment. I consider it rather unbalanced to refuse a treatment that could help you stay alive.

I was personally involved with a group that had a genuine spiritual teaching and offered spiritual growth to many people. In the late 1980s many members of the group became focused on surviving a nuclear war, thinking it was necessary to build fallout shelters. I and many people I knew watched as the movement took a detour into what can only be called a survivalist cult. This lasted for a couple of years until the bubble finally burst and the movement starting swinging back towards focusing on spiritual transformation instead of physical survival.

Why spiritual groups have not influenced society

On a more general level, I have over the years started questioning why spiritual movements and spiritual people have not had a greater impact on society. Since the 1960s, millions of people in the Western world have pursued spiritual growth and a more nonviolent approach to life. Why haven't such a large number of people had a positive impact on changing society from a materialistic approach to a more holistic approach to life?

One factor in this complex equation is that the very nature of spiritual movements divides us. I have been involved with three spiritual movements and I know people who have been involved with many others. In every spiritual movement I have heard about, you find the same pattern. In order to appeal to people, the group has to differentiate itself by offering something that you can't get anywhere else. The group makes a claim to being superior because it has the most advanced guru, the highest teachings, a unique spiritual technique or some other characteristic.

The very defining characteristic of the spiritual group is that it is special, which obviously gives the members a sense of being superior—it gives them me-esteem. The result is that millions of spiritual people are seeking to change society by converting everyone else into becoming members of their specific group. In my humble opinion, this can never work. We will never get a majority of the people in the Western world to walk around in the streets singing Indian bhajans. Nor will we get them to practice high-speed chanting in order to invoke the violet flame and transmute world karma. For that matter, we won't even get them to close their eyes 20 minutes morning and evening, as the meditation movement attempted to do. In my view, it is indeed possible to get society to accept a more spiritual outlook on life, but this can happen only if that spiritual outlook is universal. We will never succeed if we try to elevate one spiritual movement to the same dominant status as the Catholic Church had during the Dark Ages.

As long as we are caught in seeking me-esteem by making our specific movement or guru seem superior, how can we promote a universal approach to spirituality? It is hard to feel universal and superior at the same time. In my view we need to grow beyond the need to find me-esteem by being special and instead discover the true self. When you discover your true self and I discover my true self, we realize that there is only one self and we are all individual expressions of it. Incidentally, that can make you feel very special but not in comparison to other people. There is no comparison in universality.

Losing yourself in a spiritual group

Some people do not use a spiritual group to find me-esteem but to find we-esteem. The group might give them a general sense of being special because they belong to the group, but their real need is to avoid taking personal responsibility for their lives and their growth. They do this by accepting that the leader of the group has a superior status that they could never attain. They simply need to accept everything he or she says and live their lives based on all of the rules defined by the guru. As long as they live up to all of the outer requirements, they feel they have sufficient me-esteem and they essentially stop making personal decisions. The decision to join the group was the last individual decision they made.

When we are new to the spiritual path, this is a very natural and understandable reaction. You can indeed find religious and spiritual teachings that say the way to deliverance is to follow a group or a leader (incidentally, Christianity is one of them). It is a fact that due to the lack of a well-known spiritual tradition in the West (I consider Christianity a *religious*, not a *spiritual* tradition), many of the spiritual movements available today come from the East. Some Eastern spiritual gurus demand unquestioning obedience from their followers. I was personally never willing to do that because from early childhood I felt that my life is my personal responsibility.

I have observed how many people go into a state of having a sense of idolatry towards the leader of their spiritual movement. This state usually cannot last and I believe the reason is that it actually stops our genuine growth. The underlying purpose of your spiritual path is that you discover who you really are, you discover your real self.

For a time, it can be helpful to recognize that a guru has attained a state of consciousness that is higher than your own. If you develop idolatry of the guru, thinking you can never attain the same status, then this will block you from discovering your true self. The underlying truth is that each of us are extensions of the same divine being and none of us are fundamentally better or worse than others.

Jennifer is a typical example of this. She found a spiritual movement with a very strong charismatic female leader. She looked up to the guru as being specially trained over many lifetimes, meaning that Jennifer herself could never reach that same level. For years Jennifer was completely content to follow all of the rules and practice the techniques defined by her guru and she felt that by doing so, she was guaranteed to reach her spiritual goal after this lifetime. In actuality, this did give Jennifer a respite from her fear of not being good enough, a fear fueled by her Christian upbringing. Unfortunately, blindly following a guru didn't actually resolve the cause of the fear, which was that Jennifer had not accepted herself as being worthy just the way God created her. Jennifer's respite from this existential fear was bought at a price because it depended on her guru living up to a set of superhuman characteristics.

Eventually, the guru displayed some human traits and made what Jennifer considered a mistake. Jennifer's sense of me-esteem came crashing down and she ended up feeling less self-esteem than before she started following her guru. She now felt she had made a terrible mistake by submitting to the guru and she vowed never again to trust any spiritual guru or movement. What she was really doing was affirming that she would never again trust herself. This wasn't helpful to Jennifer's growth, but was this because the guru had deceived her or was it because Jennifer had not yet accepted responsibility for her own growth? Jennifer's reaction isn't the only possible one. Another typical reaction is that people build such a sense of comfortability that they think they have to stay in a particular spiritual movement and continue doing the same thing for the rest of their lives.

The first spiritual movement I became involved with promoted a form of Eastern meditation. I joined the movement when I was 18 but left it three years later because I no longer felt it gave me growth. I later found an American movement that I joined, and after a few years I decided to give up my comfortable life in Denmark and move to the United States in order to live near the headquarters of this movement (I am not mentioning names because it is not my goal to promote or criticize specific movements, gurus or persons). My time in the United States was very challenging with many difficult situations and changes, but the overall effect was to change my perspective in a way that could never have happened by staying in Denmark.

An old friend of mine, Margaret, had followed a very similar path after we had met in the meditation movement. Margaret left that movement when I did, found the second movement and also moved to the United States. Margaret also felt that the many challenges she had encountered had shifted her world view so much that 20 years felt more like several lifetimes. After Margaret moved back to Denmark, she got back together with Alice, an old friend she knew from the meditation movement. Margaret told me how she very much enjoyed talking to Alice, but one day she realized that Alice had hardly changed at all during those 20 years. Alice still followed the teachings of the meditation movement to the letter and she still believed that any day the world would wake up and acknowledge that meditation is the one solution to all problems. Margaret said she was in shock by the contrast between her own dramatic growth and the fact that Alice seemed to be exactly the same person as 20 years earlier.

My conclusion based on similar experiences is that conforming to a spiritual movement or guru does not help you attain self-esteem. After an initial period of growth, you get trapped in a closed loop. You have created a sense of we-esteem, but your illusion of worth is built on you conforming to the group or guru. Obviously, this is not coming from inside the self.

There must be a better way

As I said, most of us grew up without any experience with the spiritual path, so it is virtually inevitable that we all have to go through a phase of experimenting with what is available in the marketplace. Experimentation means something very simple: You try out different things. Some things work and some things don't work.

Unfortunately, our lack of self-esteem makes experimentation a risky business. Many people get hurt and some people get stuck for decades. I was deeply hurt by my involvement with my first spiritual movement, and I have met many people who had a similar experience.

Jennifer's story is a typical example of a person who experienced such trauma that she has spent 15 years blaming her former guru instead of realizing that she needs to take responsibility for her own path.

In contrast, I have met literally hundreds of people who experimented with gurus and movements, made mistakes but ended up taking responsibility for their path. They learned their lessons and moved on to turn the spiritual path into an upward spiral. Instead of using their experimentation to stop their growth, they used their mistakes as a way to build maturity and discernment. They became sophisticated shoppers in the religious supermarket. They started sensing that there had to be a better way, and they started looking for a deeper, more genuine approach to spirituality.

I am hoping that this book will help you move through the experimental phase without getting hurt. If you have already been hurt, I hope this book will help you heal the wounds and develop an approach that takes you towards genuine self-esteem. The simple fact is that the superficial quest for me-esteem or we-esteem can never give you genuine self-esteem. Instead, the only way to develop true self-esteem is to take a closer look at the self.

Keys from Chapter 1

◊   **Shaky self-esteem** depends on factors outside yourself, factors that can be difficult to control.

◊   **Solid self-esteem** comes from inside the self. You have the potential to control your own mind.

◊   **Solid self-esteem** is the natural state of the self. Shaky self-esteem requires a constant struggle. Removing the factors that cause shaky self-esteem will reduce the struggle.

◊   **Shaky self-esteem** is based on seeking to live up to a standard defined in the material world.

◊   Seeking to stand out from the crowd gives you **me-esteem**.

◊   Seeking to blend into a group gives you **we-esteem**. **Me-esteem** and **we-esteem** are both shaky and they are not true self-esteem.

◊   Spiritual people often have low self-esteem because they do not fit in. This can derail our spiritual path into a futile quest for **me-esteem** and **we-esteem**.

◊   **The key to solid self-esteem** is to know the self so that you realize you are a psycho-spiritual being and not a product of the material world.

2 | RECLAIMING YOUR SPIRITUAL SENSE *of* SELF

How can we find true self-esteem if our thoughts and feelings about ourselves are based on factors that are beyond our control? As just one example, look at our physical bodies. Certainly, there are things we can do to change our physical appearance, but there is a limit to how far we can go. We can't (at least not based on current knowledge) change our genes and turn brown eyes into blue. We can't change our basic body type and looks. For most of us, it is an undeniable reality that we have to find a way to live with the bodies we have received in what often seems like a lottery.

At the same time we live in a society that programs us to think our physical bodies should be evaluated based on a standard of beauty that no one can really define. The result is that very few people live up to it, and those who do only live up to it for a time. If you take this standard seriously, you might be condemned to having low self-esteem for your entire lifetime or at least for the last part of it. Is that really a way to live? If you were not one of the lucky winners of the body lottery, what can you do? Well, it depends on your outlook on life.

I have said that the key to self-esteem is to get to know the self. I have said that the key to knowing the self is to follow a spiritual path that gradually shifts your sense of self. What can a spiritual outlook do for you in terms of your feelings towards your physical body?

You are more than your body

The most universal spiritual outlook I have found says that there are two compartments in our total world. One is what we can detect with our physical senses and scientific instruments, namely the material world. Beyond that is a spiritual realm that is just as real, and in this realm live spiritual beings. In fact, we are spiritual beings who have chosen to take on physical bodies here on earth—we have taken embodiment. This means we did not suddenly come into existence at the birth of the body, nor will we disappear when the body dies.

When you accept this view, you can begin to shift your sense of self away from identification with the physical body. Thereby, you can also avoid having your self-esteem be so dependent on the looks of your body. A spiritual outlook gives you the sense that your life has a purpose that reaches beyond the body. Your body is simply a vehicle that you are using in pursuit of your long-term spiritual goals.

What are your spiritual goals? There can be many, but the most universal one is to raise your consciousness towards higher levels, eventually reaching the highest level possible here on earth—however that might be defined by a specific spiritual teaching. In universal terms, earth is a kind of learning environment designed to help us raise our consciousness. This eventually leads us to "graduate" from "Terra University." We have the potential to go through a process called the ascension, whereby we earn our permanent place in the spiritual realm. We then become "ascended masters" and can now serve as teachers for people on earth, just as there are ascended beings who serve as our teachers today.

Mystical teachings from both East and West say that this process takes more time than the life span of one physical body. We have inhabited many bodies before this one, and we may have lifetimes after this one. When we reach the highest level of consciousness possible on earth, we will no longer have to come back to a physical body.

Accepting your body

How does this view help you deal with the physical body you currently inhabit? First of all, you see that the purpose for your life is not to be admired for having a body that lives up to a temporary and artificial standard created in current society. You might not be aware of this, but just a few centuries ago the prevailing standard of beauty was quite different.

Back then most people did not have enough food, so being overweight was not an option for most women. "Ordinary" people had to work outdoors and would therefore get a tan. As a result, the ideal woman was considered to be pale and well rounded, meaning exactly the way most women look today. The skinny tan models of today would have been considered unattractive peasant women during the Renaissance. When you adopt a spiritual outlook, why even worry about your body not conforming to the ideal? Your body is a vehicle for your growth in consciousness and the looks of your body cannot in any way prevent your growth—unless you choose to let this be a hindrance.

One of the most useful concepts I have found during my spiritual search is that we each have a divine plan. Before we were born in this lifetime, we met with our spiritual teachers. These teachers are permanent residents in the spiritual realm, and many of them started by being in embodiment like us. They have gone through the process we are going through of raising their consciousness until they qualified to ascend, which is why I prefer to call them ascended masters. Together with our teachers, we created a realistic plan for what we wanted to experience, learn and do in the coming lifetime.

This plan was carefully designed based on a neutral evaluation of what has happened to us in past lifetimes, where we are in our overall progress towards a higher state of consciousness and what we want to experience on earth. Of course, as the spiritual parts of our beings enter physical bodies, we forget this divine plan, but it is quite possible for most people to get an intuitive sense of their divine plan. In fact, most spiritually minded people already have some sense of this, and they have followed their divine plans in major life decisions.

Your divine plan has many facets and one may be to teach other people. This is especially true for people who have a spiritual outlook on life. How do we teach? In life's schoolroom we first of all teach by example, we teach by how we live our lives. As spiritual people we have often chosen to be born into difficult circumstances in order to demonstrate to other people how a spiritual approach to life can help us either transcend our outer circumstances or live with them in a way that raises our consciousness. We teach by demonstrating that there is more to life than what most people were brought up to believe. This might mean that you chose to take on your current physical body as part of your divine plan. The purpose was to demonstrate that despite the looks or handicaps of your body, you can still find inner peace and a sense that your life has a sublime meaning.

Ralph was a good example of that. Confined to a wheelchair since childhood, he nevertheless radiated a sense of peace that many healthy people might envy him. Ralph didn't act like a spiritual teacher nor did he seem to see himself as one. Nevertheless, he taught me that by fully accepting what you cannot change, you will make your life so much easier than if you constantly fight against your circumstances.

Why do we so often struggle? Is it not because we have a certain expectation of what life should be, and as long as it has not been fulfilled, we don't feel we can enjoy life? We struggle to attain certain outer circumstances, only to find that they don't make us happy. Joe had grown up in a well-to-do family, had been given a car when he was 16 and a college education, but he never seemed to appreciate what he had—including a strong and healthy body—and was one of the most unhappy people I have ever met. In contrast, Ralph was one of the happiest. So how do you explain that a person in a wheelchair can be happier than one who has everything? It can only be explained by one's attitude to life. Do you accept what you cannot change and make the best of it or do you make yourself miserable by struggling against what you cannot change or what doesn't even exist outside your own mind?

A spiritual outlook can also help us do something to change our bodies. If you accept that you have lived before, you probably also accept that what you did in past lifetimes can carry over and set certain limitations for this lifetime. Most Eastern spiritual teachings call this karma, and one effect of our karma can be an illness or the looks of your body.

Changing your body

I know that some Hindu teachings portray karma as being pre-destination, meaning you can do nothing about it, but I have come to see it as a lesson. For example, a tendency to become depressed can be a sign that in a past lifetime you experienced traumatic circumstances that gave you an emotional wound and affected the way you look at life and yourself. Many spiritual teachings say we can transmute our negative karma by using spiritual tools. For example, by using appropriate tools to go deep into your psyche, you can resolve such wounds and shift your outlook on life towards a positive view. This can have positive effects on your life, as I have personally seen in many people I have met on my path. I will later describe such tools.

A spiritual outlook can also help us deal with a body that is overweight. Teachings given by our ascended teachers say that this is often caused by a past-life trauma. People put on weight because they feel emotionally vulnerable, and a layer of physical bulk gives a sense of being protected or being isolated from the world. I once worked with Dana, a young woman who was grossly overweight despite following a diet that should have caused her to be as thin as a supermodel. After spending her twenties trying out every weight-loss fad that came around, she finally decided to go into therapy and eventually uncovered a very deep trauma. After she healed the trauma, her need for protection disappeared and her weight started disappearing as well. The most important effect of a spiritual outlook is that it can help you accept your body as the ideal vehicle for your personal growth in this lifetime.

This will help you free your attention and energy from being preoccupied with the body. You can then free your mind to focus on other aspects of life. Instead of seeking to build self-esteem based on the body, you can seek more effective ways. In fact, you can begin to increase your awareness of the self that is not the body but only uses the body as a vehicle. This opens up many productive avenues for growth.

Selves left over from past lives

I no longer remember how old I was when I first heard about reincarnation. I do know that I accepted it instantly because it explained something I had observed. Even as a child I was very much aware that we human beings are psychological beings and that everything we do depends on our individual psychological "topography." For example, my father and his older brother had a typical sibling rivalry and spent most of their lives in competition with each other, which really made our family lives much more difficult than necessary.

I knew that I myself had certain psychological wounds. For example, I was extremely shy and felt very bad about being laughed at or making a fool of myself in a public setting. Such deep patterns simply could not have been created in just one lifetime. This observation has been reinforced by meeting so many spiritual seekers who had far more difficult childhoods than I did. I had such an easy and harmonious childhood that there is simply no way I could have become so wounded in this lifetime alone.

If you take a quick look at the history of this planet, you can see that most of us have probably had some very difficult past lives. We have likely been affected by wars and have been killed, lost family members or seen our entire lives being bombed into ruins. We may also have spent lifetimes as part of the downtrodden masses who slaved to provide privileges for a small elite. I have met many people who have felt that they had been involved with religious persecutions and had been tortured or burned at the stake for having nonstandard beliefs.

This leads to a potentially very productive conclusion, namely that in past lives we have built up at least two different selves and that they might be working against each other. One of these selves might make it impossible for us to find true self-esteem. This view is supported by many spiritual teachers and some modern psychologists. The reason this realization can be so productive is that we now get a different view on how to attain self-esteem.

The big problem in our modern culture is that we have not been given a deeper understanding of the self, which means we think the self is one, homogenous whole. As a result, we think that the only way to build self-esteem is to seek to improve our outer situation instead of doing something about our inner situation. Let me give you a different view of the self and then explain how this can set your quest for self-esteem on a much more constructive track.

I take a universal approach to spirituality. I have studied a wide range of religious and spiritual teachings, from Christianity and Buddhism to the teachings of the ascended masters, and I don't believe any of them have a monopoly on truth. When I study a teaching, I always look for the universal elements and you can find them in all traditions.

The human self and the pure self

Most of the spiritual seekers I know grew up in a Christian culture and most of them have either abandoned Christianity or have a conflicted relationship with this religion. Many people I know felt official Christianity did not answer their deeper questions about life but always referred to a standard doctrine. My friends from a Catholic background said the standard answer to their questions was "It's a mystery." As a result, they simply stopped asking questions in church and looked elsewhere for answers. I personally remember going through the preparations for my Lutheran confirmation, and I quickly realized the priest who taught us had no answers beyond standard doctrines. I couldn't understand why you would choose to become a priest if you had not found better answers to life's deeper questions.

Personally, I see many universal elements in the teachings of Jesus, and I would like to use some of them to illustrate the issue of the two selves. In the Gospel of John, there is a situation where Jesus is talking to a Pharisee named Nicodemus. Jesus tells him that in order to enter the kingdom of heaven, you must be born again. Nicodemus asks how this can happen, for how can you enter your mother's womb a second time?

Jesus then makes it clear that what he is talking about is a spiritual or psychological rebirth. To me, what Jesus is saying between the lines is that being spiritually reborn means to shift your sense of self towards a higher state. Jesus then makes an intriguing statement, namely that the only person who can ascend back to heaven is the person that descended from heaven. Let us restate that by saying that only the self that descended from the spiritual realm can ascend back to the spiritual realm. In other words, according to Jesus, the key to graduating from earth is to shift your sense of self back to the pure state in which it first descended. As he said, unless we become as little children we cannot enter the kingdom.

When I combine this with reincarnation, I see that in the distant past we started the process of taking embodiment on earth as a particular self. I will later describe this self, but for now I want to keep it simple so I am leaving it open. This self faced a rather complicated task because it came out of the spiritual realm, which is very different from the material world. In order to use a dense physical body, the self that descended had to create another self that could integrate with a physical body.

I have pieced together this idea from different sources, and I believe it illustrates our basic dilemma as human beings. We have seen that the physical body is simply a vehicle that you use here on earth. It is comparable to a car, which you get into, drive to a destination and then get out of. You never get confused and start thinking that you are your car and cannot leave it behind.

Unfortunately, many of us have forgotten that we are spiritual beings. We have come to identify ourselves with or as a physical body living in a particular situation on earth. How could this happen?

Many spiritual and religious teachings talk about the concept that we have forgotten who we are as spiritual beings and have come to see ourselves as human beings. The Old Testament has the story of the Garden of Eden and how Adam and Eve were cast out after eating a forbidden fruit. According to ascended master teachings, this is a metaphor for a fall in the level of our consciousness.

Buddhism also talks about us having lost our original sense of being connected to all life, which has caused us to forget that the Buddha nature is within us. Instead, we see life as a perpetual struggle, but the struggle is created in our own minds. Jesus talked about a consciousness of death and a consciousness of life. Like the Buddha, Jesus said that the kingdom of God is within us, meaning it is a state of mind.

The explanation I have pieced together is that we descended into embodiment as a pure self. In order to interact with the physical body, we had to create a self in this world. If we compare this to getting into a car, we can say that the spiritual self got into the human self and then the combination of the two selves got into first one and then many other physical bodies.

Over many lifetimes in the bloody past of earth, we were forced to react to very dramatic and very traumatic situations. What reacted to these situations was the human self, and over time this self grew more complex and more powerful. Eventually it swallowed up all of our conscious attention, so we completely forgot that at our core is a pure self. The pure self did not come from this world and thus cannot be changed by anything that happens in this world. However, when we look at ourselves through the filter of the human self, we think we are nothing more than human beings.

The central human dilemma is that we have forgotten our spiritual origin, we have lost the sense of being a pure self from the spiritual realm. The very core of the spiritual path, as I see it, is to return to the original state of purity, because only the pure self can graduate from earth and ascend back to the spiritual realm. What can this tell us about our quest for self-esteem?

The human self cannot feel self-esteem

Again, let me refer to an enigmatic statement made by Jesus. There is a situation where Jesus is telling a young man to follow him and be his disciple. The man says that his father has just died and he wants to go home and bury him first. Jesus then says: "Let the dead bury their dead." Obviously, corpses do not run around and bury other corpses, so what did Jesus mean? My conclusion is that Jesus is using the word "dead" in two distinct ways. The boy's father was physically dead and the people burying him were dead in a spiritual sense because they had forgotten that they were spiritual beings.

Jesus also said that if you seek to hold on to your life, you shall lose it, but if you are willing to lose your life for his sake, you will have eternal life. He also said he is the way, the truth and the life. I interpret this to mean that Jesus came to show us the potential for returning to the state of purity with which we first descended into physical embodiment. We do this by reawakening to the fact that we are still the pure self that descended and that we forgot this because we started identifying ourselves with the human self.

How do we awaken? By letting the human self die bit by bit, thus lessening the hold it has on our conscious awareness. When the magnetic pull of the human self has been reduced to a critical degree, we will be spiritually reborn and shift into a higher sense of self. The eighth-century Buddhist teacher, Padma Sambhava, who is credited with bringing Buddhism to Tibet, has written a very intriguing treatise that talks about the need to cultivate a pure form of awareness. It is called *Self-liberation Through Seeing with Naked Awareness* and its aim is to help you snap out of the mindset that we were brought up to see as normal but which most spiritual teachers see as a very persuasive collective illusion.

The only way for you to attain a true form of self-esteem is to shift your sense of identity, your sense of self, until you can see and accept yourself as a spiritual being. You will then have true self-knowledge and you will experience yourself as a beautiful being with an inherent worth, seeing that your worth does not depend on anything on earth. You are worthy in and of yourself, you are worthy because of the way you were created.

Obviously none of us were brought up with this understanding and that means we were left with only one option, namely to pursue self-esteem through the human self. The problem is that the human self was created as a reaction to conditions here on earth. It can never come to see itself as a spiritual being and it can never accept that it has inherent worth. It can only see itself as a material being, and thus it can only see self-esteem as a product of living up to certain material conditions.

One might say that the beginning of the spiritual path is when we realize that we can indeed overcome the sense of self that makes us believe we are material beings. As long as your self-esteem is based on certain conditions here on earth, it will inevitably be threatened by other conditions on earth. As I was growing up, I was always very disturbed by many of the things I saw around me or learned about history.

How could human beings possibly commit such incredible atrocities as wars and the Holocaust? I still remember the raw shock of seeing photos of concentration camp inmates that looked like walking skeletons. I could not understand how such things were possible until I found teachings given by the ascended masters. These beings have completed the final exam on earth, so they are no longer blinded by the human consciousness. They see the bigger picture that we do not see.

Human, know thy planet

The ascended masters explain that there are many planets in the material world with intelligent life. On most of these planets the inhabitants have raised their individual and collective consciousness far beyond the level seen on earth. Many of the limitations and atrocities we see on this planet simply do not exist there. Earth is one of the lower planets in the cosmos and that is why we do see so many examples of "man's inhumanity to man."

This knowledge helped me see that I had grown up with an unrealistic expectation about life on earth. I have met many spiritual people who have an inner, intuitive sense for what life is like on a higher planet or in a higher realm. Many of us volunteered to take embodiment on earth in order to help raise this planet, but until we actually came into a physical body, we did not understand how difficult it is to maintain a spiritual sense of identity on a planet as dense as earth.

I have over the years done a lot of work on identifying and healing my deepest traumas. The deepest trauma I have so far identified is the sense of coming to earth with the best of intentions only to experience how I was viciously attacked by people who did not want to be reminded that they are spiritual beings. I believe many seekers have the same scars deep within their souls, and in many cases we have created a sophisticated human self in order to deal with this trauma.

Once you understand that the earth is a very low planet, you can see why you cannot build true self-esteem based on living up to conditions found here. If you allow your human self to run your quest for self-esteem, you might think that the way to have self-esteem is to have lots of money. Making lots of money is not easy and there may be many obstacles that could cause you to fall short of the goal. How much money do you need in order to build a secure sense of self-esteem? Based on some of the rich people you see on television, one might suspect you can never have enough money to feel really at peace with yourself.

Of course, even if you did get the money, you know there are people who might attempt to take it from you. Or you might lose it through other factors that are completely beyond your control, such as a natural disaster or a financial crisis. Many rich people have their lives consumed by making money and protecting their money and it doesn't seem to give them lasting self-esteem. Of course, we all know there will come a time when you will have to leave the body and the money behind.

The conclusion I reach is that we can never attain true and lasting self-esteem through the human self. The only way to build self-esteem is to pursue the spiritual path. The problem is that unless we understand the need to let the human self die, we can easily be misled into following the spiritual path based on the needs, the fears and the perceptions of the human self. This will not lead us to self-esteem and there is a specific reason for that.

The division of the human self

The key to spiritual growth is that we shift from a human to a spiritual sense of self. It took me many years to grasp this fact, and the reason is that many spiritual teachings either do not teach this or they teach it in a veiled form. This caused me to spend a lot of time and much effort on what was essentially a wild goose chase. I was seeking to use a spiritual teaching to raise or perfect my human self, thinking that if only my human self would conform to a spiritual standard, then it would be able to get me into heaven.

For years I was aware that we have a human self but I saw it as a homogenous whole. It took me a while to understand that the human self has a fundamental and inescapable division. When the pure self first descended into a physical body on earth, it saw itself as an extension of a higher self in the spiritual realm. The pure self had a sense of being one with something greater than itself and this gave it a form of self-esteem that does not depend on anything in the material world.

The human self was created in this world and it does not define itself as an extension of a being in the spiritual realm. It defines itself as a separate being existing in the material world. Consequently, the human self can build self-esteem only by using conditions in this world. We can say that the world view of the pure self is based on oneness whereas for the human self it is based on separation. How do you leave oneness and go into separation? By a division into at least two opposites.

Many spiritual teachings talk about two basic polarities, but the most well-known is Taoism. Most people know the Tai Chi, the circle that is divided into a black field and a white field that seem to swirl into each other. The deeper symbolism is that everything in the world is created from the interplay of two forces or principles, namely an outgoing force and a contracting force. Any form is created by both forces, but for the form to be sustainable, there must be a dynamic balance between them. If this balance is lost, the two forces become opposites that destroy each other instead of being complementary forces that create new life. This is why the Buddha talked about the Middle Way and Jesus talked about avoiding the broad (divided) way and finding the strait and narrow (undivided) way.

Everything that we do involves both the expansive and the contracting force. How do we personally achieve balance between them? This can be done only by the pure self because only this self can see oneness. When you know that behind all material phenomena is an underlying oneness, you see that the two forces spring from oneness and are complementary. When you cannot see oneness, you think the two forces are opposites and you will inevitably take one of them too far, destroying balance. The human self can never balance the two forces, and this explains why so many people swing from one extreme form of behavior to another.

Because the human self sprang from separation, it has a fundamental division into two or more opposing factions. In terms of self-esteem, there are two basic divisions. One part of the human self knows it is a separate being and thus it can never achieve true self-esteem. This part is constantly projecting at your conscious mind that you are worthless, fundamentally flawed and that there is nothing you can do about it.

Another part of the human self says: "Not so fast, I can build a sense of self-esteem by using the conditions in the material world. If I live up to a standard or if I am better than other people, I will have worth." This part is projecting at your conscious mind that you must constantly be doing something to increase your worth according to an earthly standard. You must constantly be comparing yourself and others to this standard, hoping you do better than others. Perhaps you must even seek to put them down in order to raise up yourself. The human self cannot see that these divisions were created as a pair and that one cannot exist without the other.

The human self feels worthless but it believes that if only it can live up to a standard in an ultimate way, then the worthless part of itself will die and the worthy part will take over and feel secure. In reality, this can never happen, which is why you see so many people pursuing status but never feeling it is enough.

I earlier mentioned how I was given a ride by Stephen, who then proceeded to tell me how important of a person he was. This taught me that people who seek to build up outer status do so to cover over the insecurity they feel deep inside. As a child I could not understand how Hitler could claim the Germans were superior and the Jews inferior. When I became older and read about Hitler's personal psychology, it became obvious that he was driven to seek superiority because of his inner sense of inferiority.

Such examples taught me that people are often using superiority to cover over their inferiority. As the saying goes, those who really are superior don't need to show it. If your quest for self-esteem is driven by these two factions of the human self, you will never achieve true self-esteem and your life will be a frantic pursuit of an impossible goal.

No matter what you do on earth, you will never silence the worthless part of your human self. It will always have a deficit and the worthy part will seek to compensate for it by making you *do* more or *own* more. There is only one way out of this rat race, and it is to return to the pure sense of self with which you originally descended. Returning to purity requires balance.

The Middle Way

You may already know the story of the Buddha, but here is a short summary. The Buddha was born as a prince who lived a very privileged and protected life. His father kept him in the palace and the palace gardens where he never encountered lack, ugliness or people who were poor, ill or old. He literally did not know that our bodies will eventually die. One day the prince walked outside the palace grounds and came upon an old man who was close to death. At that moment, he realized that life in this world is only temporary and that death is a certainty.

The young man instantly shifted from the one extreme of leading a comfortable material life to the opposite of wanting to deny the temporary pleasures of this world and find a more permanent form of existence. He left the palace behind and joined a group of ascetics who practiced very strict disciplines, including starving themselves almost to death and sitting in meditation for so long that birds built nests in their hair. After six years of this extreme lifestyle, the Buddha had an epiphany.

He saw the reality that his asceticism would never get him to his goal. He realized that both the materialistic and the ascetic lifestyles were driven by factions of the human self. He then saw that the only way to a permanent existence is the Middle Way.

The essence of the Middle Way is to shift your sense of self away from the divisions of the human self and back to its pure state where you find a natural balance between the two creative forces. Before the Buddha saw the Middle Way, he was caught in the pattern I have described. He was seeking to solve a problem created by the human self by using the conditions in this world.

Let me relate this to our quest for self-esteem. The basic world view of the human self is that it is a separate being. This separateness causes the human self to gravitate towards one of two extremes. When we identify ourselves with the human self, we gravitate towards one of these extremes and we fail to see any other way to live. We fall into the pattern of seeking me-esteem by competing with others or seeking we-esteem by conforming to a group. The net effect is that our lives become a constant struggle. I believe that both Jesus, Buddha and many other spiritual teachers have come to offer us a way beyond this ongoing human struggle.

Whenever we go into the extreme of conformity or the extreme of competition, we create an imbalance. It is a natural law that imbalance is not sustainable. This is taught in Taoism in the form of yin and yang, but it is also found in many other spiritual teachings. I have already mentioned that both the Buddha and Jesus taught the need for balance.

After many years of taking an unbalanced approach to the spiritual path, I finally understood why balance is so important. By reading books about popular science, such as *The Tao of Physics*, I learned about the second law of thermodynamics. This law states that in a closed system, disorder will increase until all structures break down and the system returns to the lowest possible energy state. Another way to say this is that a closed system has a fundamental imbalance between the two creative forces. This destroys the complementarity and turns the two forces into opposites. The conflict or tension between them causes all structures in the system to break down.

It wasn't a big leap for my fertile imagination to see that the human mind can become a closed system. The human self is, by its very nature, a closed system because it sees itself as separated from the spiritual realm and from other people. Any action we take from the human self is imbalanced and such an action creates an energy impulse that is sent out into the universe. This is what many spiritual teachings call karma.

The impulse cycles through the universe and eventually comes back to us, but what comes back is not simply what we sent out, because the universe multiplies all of our efforts. When the impulse returns to us in a multiplied form, it will impact our lives. In order to counteract this influence, we will have to take an even stronger action. In other words, one unbalanced action leads to a more extreme return, which then makes it necessary for us to become even more unbalanced in order to deal with the return.

The result of this process is that the human self creates a downward spiral. An example of this on the personal level is when people get into substance abuse and end up alienating all the people around them, losing their jobs, destroying their health and eventually attempting or committing suicide. Even groups of people, nations and civilizations can create downward spirals that lead to disaster. Look at how the Roman Empire disintegrated from within until it was overrun by an external enemy. Look at how Hitler led the German nation into its ultimate defeat at the end of the war. One might argue that our Western civilization has created its own downward spiral and it is only a matter of when the breakdown will happen.

The underlying mechanism is that once you become a closed system, you think there is only one way to respond to every situation. Thus, you will go further and further into extremes until something breaks down. What breaks down is the illusion that the human self is capable of getting us where we want to go in life. This breakdown of illusion is actually a grace because it can open our minds to a spiritual teacher who can show us a better approach.

If you are submitting yourself to a group, you are being unbalanced because you are not making your own decisions. Something will come up that will threaten your sense that all is well. You can counteract this in various ways, but it requires an effort. This effort creates an impulse that will be returned by the universe as a stronger threat to your sense of comfortability (if you sow the wind, you will reap the whirlwind). This spiral can continue until the mental effort of conforming to the group becomes too much and you feel like you can't do this anymore. This is what I saw in myself when I left the meditation movement, and I also saw it in several other people who left at the same time. I have since met many spiritual people who spend a lot of mental and emotional energy on defending their guru or spiritual movement as the only one for them. Yet if it really was the only one for you, why would you have to defend staying there? So maybe it is time to go within and tune in to what is the next level of your divine plan?

If you are seeking to become more special than others, this also requires a mental effort. The effort to become superior will create a karmic return that will threaten your sense of being special. You now have to exert an even bigger mental effort to become more superior, and this can escalate until the mental effort eats up your life and you realize this can't go on.

I used to think that this breakdown was unpleasant and should be avoided. I now understand that it is actually a positive force that always works towards our growth. It is only when we go into an extreme and resist moving on that we experience a breakdown. The breakdown can shatter our sense of we-esteem or me-esteem. I have seen how this can hurt people and I have certainly experienced it myself, but I hope this book will help you see that this experience is an opportunity to take your path to a higher level. By becoming more aware of how the human self works, you can learn to move on before you go so far into extremes that a breakdown happens. It is always better to have a break-through than a break-down.

Keys from Chapter 2

◊ **Accepting that you are a spiritual being** helps you avoid the treadmill of seeking me-esteem based on the looks and abilities of your physical body.

◊ **Accepting reincarnation** helps you see that you have had many lifetimes to create a very complex human self, a self that is programmed to seek esteem in the material world.

◊ **You have two selves**. The pure self was created in the spiritual realm and descended into the material world. The human self was created in this world and can only react to conditions here.

◊ **The human self** has a fundamental division that prevents it from feeling true self-esteem. The human self always has many divisions, but each division has two polarities that cannot exist without each other.

◊ **The human self** wants you to believe that if you live up to a standard defined here on earth, you will eliminate the unworthy self and the worthy self will win. Neither self can exist without the other so the quest for this form of esteem is futile.

◊ **Striving to be on the Middle Way** means transcending the duality of the human self.

3 | CLEARING YOUR ENERGY FIELD

Why can it be difficult to shift from a sense of self that is limited to one that gives us true self-esteem? What makes it so hard to pull ourselves away from the magnetism of the human self and its view of the world? There are two main factors that keep us trapped in the human self, and in this chapter I will describe one of them and how it impacts our quest for self-esteem. I will start by examining why it can be so painful for us to be disappointed by a spiritual movement, teacher or belief system because this will help clarify what ties us to the human self.

We always attract the spiritual teacher we need

When we start a love relationship, we normally go through what psychologists call the "honeymoon phase." We are convinced that because we have met this wonderful person, the relationship will be "happily ever after." What actually happens is that we are fooled by the human self into believing that because the other person is so unique, we can achieve me-esteem and we-esteem without having to change our sense of self. As several books on relationships describe, there will inevitably come a point when the illusion is shattered and we realize that for a relationship to work we must be willing to change ourselves.

When we find our first spiritual movement or spiritual teacher, we likewise have a honeymoon phase. Again, we feel we have attained a new sense of me-esteem and we-esteem by becoming a member of this superior movement. We think we can make progress without having to shift our sense of self, without having to let the human self die. We only need to practice the techniques and follow the rules defined by our guru.

As I have described, we often start by using somewhat artificial measures, such as past lives or psychics, in order to build me-esteem. When we become aware this does not build solid self-esteem, we can then take our path to a new level, which I call the "doing phase." This phase can take many different forms, but the common denominator is that we have now recognized that making spiritual progress requires a determined and sustained effort. We are no longer looking for a quick-fix but a more long-term commitment. We are no longer looking for feel-good spirituality but something that really helps us change our lives. We might even have realized that if we look for a quick-fix, we get a slow fizzle.

There is an old saying I have found very useful: "When the student is ready, the teacher appears." This saying has helped me develop a more constructive approach to spiritual growth than what I had at the age of 18. Let me illustrate it by talking about my reaction to leaving the first spiritual movement I belonged to. The meditation movement made the claim that it had a form of meditation that was unique, and by practicing it regularly one would attain a higher state of consciousness in just a few years. This claim was not based on any experiential evidence. The movement had a lot of scientific studies showing positive effects of meditation, but there was no one who had actually attained this higher state of consciousness as a result of meditating. Instead, the main claim was based on another claim, namely that the founder of the movement had reached an enlightened state of consciousness and therefore meditation was effective because he said so. You can find similar claims in many spiritual and religious movements. For that matter, the Marxists I met in college had a similar belief in the infallibility of Marx and Engels.

At first I was swept up in the very tangible enthusiasm felt in the meditation movement in those days and this was my honeymoon phase. After a couple of years, I started realizing something simply wasn't right. I could never fully believe that meditation in itself was enough for a person to reach enlightenment. I sensed I would also have to look at my psychological issues. I also experienced that, for me, meditation had negative side effects. Finally, I started seeing that the guru of the movement had certain human idiosyncrasies. For example, he was clearly affected by an Indian world view and had a lower respect for women than I was accustomed to from growing up in Denmark.

All of this came together and I finally left the movement. After leaving, I had a couple of years where I didn't want to have anything to do with any spiritual teaching, and I consequently felt like I was in a vacuum. I also had a lot of anger, and I did what the human self always does: I directed it at something outside myself, and the meditation movement was the obvious scapegoat. In reality, as is always the case, I was angry with myself. Why? I was angry because I felt I had been stupid for believing in the exaggerated promises made by the meditation movement. There was also another reason though. Joining the movement had caused me to get quite a bit of negative reaction from my family and at the university I attended. I had dealt with that by feeling that I was simply more spiritual than those who were criticizing me, and the proof was that I was a member of this sophisticated movement that would save the world. I had used the movement to build both we-esteem and me-esteem, but it was all contingent upon me being an enthusiastic member.

When I left, my esteem came crashing down and I now felt even worse than before I joined the movement. I wished that feeling would go away, but because I was so focused on blaming the movement, I thought the only way to have avoided the pain was to not have been involved with the movement in the first place. Since I couldn't undo the past, I now felt stuck and I refused to accept personal responsibility for my situation.

A few years ago, I read Elizabeth Gilbert's book *Eat, Pray, Love*. She describes her own involvement with an Indian guru but doesn't mention the movement by name. I got curious and looked it up on the internet, and in the process I came across a discussion forum for ex-members of that movement. Upon reading their testimonies, I saw that they were going through exactly the same feelings that I had experienced with my first movement.

I have since seen that my experience was very similar to what probably millions of Westerners have experienced by being involved with a spiritual movement, which is why I am using it as an example. How could I have reacted to that first experience in a more mature and constructive manner? The first thing I could have done was to ask myself this question:

"Why did I magnetize myself to that particular movement and what can this teach me about myself?" This question is the natural outcome of understanding the old saying that when the student is ready, the teacher appears. If you give that statement a twist, you see that we are always ready for some kind of teacher.

At any given time, I am at a certain level of consciousness. At that level, I have certain lessons to learn and I have certain psychological conditions to overcome. As a linear illustration, imagine a spiral staircase. The staircase starts at the ground level where I have an unobstructed vision of the surrounding landscape. When I go down the staircase, I gradually lose that vision until I can see nothing but the step on which I am standing.

This symbolizes what happened to the pure self as it reinforced the human self. For each time the pure self took a step down the spiral staircase, it accepted a certain illusion created by the dualistic vision of the human self. In the beginning, the pure self could still see the light at the top of the staircase. As it went further down, its vision became more limited until it could no longer see the light but only the stairwell itself. This was when the pure self started believing it is a human self.

At any moment, I am at a particular step of my personal staircase. I have accepted certain illusions of my human self and these illusions limit my vision. The result is that I can recognize only a certain type of spiritual teacher. I cannot see a teacher who teaches at a much higher level of consciousness, I can see only a teacher that corresponds to my own level. The beauty of this is that the teacher I can see is precisely the best teacher for helping me learn what I need to learn in order to move to a higher level.

The esteem equation

The trick is, of course, that in order to move to a higher level of consciousness, I have to learn the lessons at my present level, and those lessons will not be obvious. The reason for that is that my limited vision will prevent me from seeing what I need to learn. In order to learn the lesson, I have to raise my vision; and in order to raise my vision, I need experience.

When I found the meditation movement, it was my goal to reach a higher level of consciousness. I bought into the idea that I could achieve this by meditating. That belief was a product of my level of consciousness, which wasn't very mature. At the time, I wasn't ready to accept two things, namely that the spiritual path is a life-long commitment and that it requires a lot of work on your personal psychology.

Instead, I could only accept the far more simplistic view that there was a quick way to reach enlightenment and that it could be done without too much work and certainly without looking too hard at the beam in my own eye. Why wasn't I ready for this more mature approach? Because my self-esteem was far too low at the time. Self-esteem is a product of getting in touch with your pure self. At the time I only had occasional glimpses of my higher self, but my everyday consciousness was largely dominated by my human self.

The human self can only have me-esteem or we-esteem. Because they are based on conditions in this world, they are easily threatened. This causes us to face a very delicate balancing act as we begin to walk the spiritual path. The equation is simple. In order to function, you have to have a certain amount of esteem. If your esteem is too low, you become discouraged and you might give up on the spiritual path or life.

The esteem coming from the human self is based on an illusion. This illusion buys us a sense of esteem, but it also blocks our spiritual growth by keeping us tied to a certain level of consciousness. In order to move closer to our pure state of self, we simply have to shed the illusions of the human self. As we shed an illusion, we will inevitably lose the esteem based on the illusion. If our loss of esteem would be too great to bear, we will—subconsciously that is—resist letting go of an illusion as a simple survival mechanism.

Of course, once we do let go of an illusion, we feel much freer, but we won't know that until we have let go. The human self will always hold on to its illusions as if it were a matter of life and death. The combination of these mechanisms can explain why we are susceptible to the belief that we can make spiritual progress without letting go of our dearest illusions. Spiritual progress really comes down to how well we deal with the balance between the pain of losing esteem and the joy of shedding an illusion.

When I found the meditation movement, my sense of esteem was very fragile. I would not have been able to handle seeing a major problem in my personal psychology. I would have felt that if I had such problems, it would be devastating to my esteem balance. As a result of this, I magnetized myself to a spiritual movement that promised me I could reach enlightenment without looking at my psychology. The teacher that appeared was exactly the teacher I was ready for—because I could not have recognized a higher teacher. What was the real lesson I needed to learn? It was not what it appeared to be, namely that I could reach enlightenment by following this teacher. On the contrary, the lesson was that you will never reach enlightenment by following an external teacher because enlightenment is an internal condition. It can come about only by me looking at and transcending each and every illusion that took me down the spiral staircase.

In reality, I was very close to being able to accept this higher level of personal responsibility. I was ready to consciously acknowledge the fact that there is no quick-fix and that the spiritual path is a long-term commitment that requires a lot of work. I was also ready to recognize that I wanted a spiritual teacher who would not make empty promises but who would help me overcome my illusions. This leads to another question: how will we recognize with our outer minds that we are ready for a higher teacher?

Letting go and receiving direction

The saying that "when the student is ready, the teacher appears" has several layers of meaning. One aspect is our divine plans, and I envision my personal divine plan as a track or timetable that is running in the background. This plan has certain points where I need to change direction in life, for example by finding (or leaving) a certain spiritual teaching. When one of these points is reached, I will receive some outer sign of the step I am meant to take. The big question is whether my conscious mind can recognize this.

Will I consciously see what is in my divine plan, or will I cling to one of my illusions in order to maintain my fragile esteem? You can be ready for a teacher at the higher levels of your mind without recognizing it at the conscious level. This was clearly the case for me after I left the meditation movement. Why did I spend two miserable years feeling like I was in a spiritual vacuum? Because at the conscious level I was not able and willing to acknowledge what kind of teacher I wanted. I had not been willing to step up to a higher level where I would take a greater degree of responsibility for my personal path. We could also say that I had not looked at my experience with the meditation movement and asked myself what I needed to learn about myself. Thus, I simply could not recognize and accept the next teacher and I felt abandoned and alone.

I have since learned that we are never abandoned by our spiritual teachers—and I am here talking about the teachers in the spiritual realm who helped us make our divine plans. Our divine plans will take us smoothly from one earthly teaching to the next, but only if we fulfill our part of the bargain. There are two conditions to fulfill:

- In order for us to see the next teaching, we must let go of the old one. You simply cannot look in two directions at the same time. You cannot look backwards and forwards at the same time. Until you let go of one teacher, teaching or movement, you cannot recognize the next one. In order to let go, we must forgive and we must take responsibility for learning the lesson we needed to learn from the previous teacher. You need to ask yourself why you were attracted to that movement and what that says about your psychology.

- Our minds must be open enough to receive an intuitive direction from our higher selves. This means there cannot be so much turmoil in our minds that we never have a quiet moment. It is always in the silent moments that we get intuitive insights. Intuition does not like to compete with the analytical mind or obsessive emotions.

The first condition is what the Buddha called an attachment. The second is a matter of how much noise we have in our minds. Intuition is like a radio. In order to receive intuitive insights from your higher self, you have to attune your conscious mind to the right station. If there is too much static, you simply cannot get a clear signal. To summarize, here are the main points I have talked about in this chapter:

• To let go of an illusion usually causes emotional pain. The more the illusion has given us esteem, the more painful it will be to let it go.

• It can be difficult to let go of a teacher and to stop looking back.

• Our minds can have so much turmoil that we cannot get a clear intuitive direction.

The explanation behind all of these problems can be summed up with one word: *energy*, whereby I mean mental and emotional, or psychic, energy.

The pain we feel by losing our sense of me-esteem or we-esteem is caused by psychic energy that has accumulated in our subconscious minds. This energy literally forms a magnetic pull on our conscious minds that makes it more difficult for us to let go of an illusion. We cannot consciously let go of an illusion, although we are ready to let go at higher levels of our psyches. If we are forced to give up the illusion, we can be plunged into unbearable pain without realizing that the pain is caused by psychic energy. In order to explain this mechanism, we need to understand a new model of the human mind.

A new model of the mind

The model I will outline here comes directly from our universal spiritual teachers, whom I call the ascended masters. I first heard about ascended masters a couple of years after I had left the meditation movement. After I had processed my experience and let go of my anger, I was open to a new kind of spiritual teacher, one who had walked the spiral staircase and graduated from earth. I didn't want a teacher who was simply higher on the staircase than me, I wanted one who was beyond the staircase and no longer had limited vision. And when the student is ready, the ascended teacher appears.

I have now studied the teachings of the ascended masters for almost 30 years. For the last 10 years I have been fortunate to work directly with these masters to bring forth new and original teachings. These teachings can be found on my websites.

The ascended masters teach that we live in a world that is made from one basic substance. This base energy has no form in itself, but it can be stirred into taking on any form. What causes the base energy to take on a particular form is that a thought matrix is superimposed upon the energy through the mind of a self-aware being. The process of creating our world began with one self-aware being. This is what most people would call God, but the ascended masters often talk about the "Creator." The Creator has not created every aspect of our world. In fact, our total world has several levels or layers. On each level there is a group of self-aware beings who serve as co-creators along with the Creator. The Creator created the first level of the world of form and sent self-aware extensions into this world as co-creators. These beings then created the next level of the world and sent extensions of themselves into that level. This process has continued, and the material world is simply the latest extension of it.

The material world was created by self-aware beings at the level above ours, namely the lowest level of the spiritual realm. They then sent us into this world, and our purpose is to serve as co-creators. Our spiritual "parents" created the world from the outside and we are meant to co-create it from the inside. We have the capacity of mind to form a mental matrix and to superimpose it upon the base energy, causing this energy to take on the form we envision. We can qualify or misqualify the basic energy by using our minds.

The ascended masters explain that we were created in the spiritual realm. We were created as self-aware beings with a divine individuality, called the I AM Presence. This individuality exists in the spiritual realm, which is made from energies that are much higher than the energies of the material world. This is an important concept because it means that nothing that has ever happened to you on earth has destroyed or even changed your I AM Presence. Your divine individuality is intact and whole. The real basis for your personal sense of self-esteem is the individuality anchored in your I AM Presence. Acquiring true self-esteem is a matter of experiencing this individuality instead of the human individuality we have all built here on earth.

What is the self that can experience this divine individuality? It is what I have called the pure self. This self is an extension of the spiritual self that is sent into the material world in order to co-create through a physical body. When this pure self first took embodiment, it did not have the full awareness of the spiritual self. It had a pointlike sense of self, but it did know that it was connected to something greater than itself.

The key concept to understand here is that the spiritual self, the I AM Presence, can never see itself as anything but a spiritual being. It can never forget its divine individuality. The spiritual self cannot fit itself into a physical body and identify itself with and as the body. This means that the I AM Presence cannot experience the material world from the inside and thus it cannot co-create this world from the inside.

In order to fulfill its role of co-creating this world, the spiritual self created an extension of itself. This pure self has no built-in individuality. Thus, it can indeed descend into a physical body and it can come to identify itself as a human being on earth. The pure self literally is what it thinks it is; it is what it sees itself as being. In its natural state, the pure self is simply pure awareness. It needs no individuality because in the pure state, the individuality of the spiritual self will shine through it.

The pure self has the ability to create and enter a human self. Once it is inside such a separate self, it will "forget" its spiritual identity and origin. That is why most people on earth have forgotten that they are spiritual beings and accept that they are limited by the prevailing definition of what it means to be a human being. Have you ever considered why athletes are able to run faster and jump higher today than in the past? It is not simply a matter of physical ability but a matter of moving beyond the mental barriers for what we think is humanly possible.

The pure self is designed to take on a physical body, which is made from energies that are far more dense than the energies of the spiritual realm. Because of the density of material energy, it is almost inevitable that we will go through the process of "forgetting" our spiritual origin and come to identify ourselves as human beings. Because we did come from a higher realm, though, we can never fully lose our longing for something more than the material world. This becomes our lifeline to awakening from the "sleep" of the human identity.

What is the purpose of this forgetting and awakening? One aspect is that this helps the spiritual self grow. The I AM Presence learns how the material world works and it learns how it can express its co-creative abilities. As we awaken, the pure self becomes an open door for the higher energies of the spiritual realm to stream into the material world, and in the long run this helps raise the material world until it eventually goes through a shift and becomes part of the spiritual realm.

The four levels of the human self

How do we co-create? The driving force behind our co-creative abilities is energy. The entire material world is created from spiritual energy that has been lowered in vibration. Once lowered to the spectrum of material energy, the formless energy has then been organized into certain matrices that we perceive as material forms. This happened because self-aware beings used their minds to impose mental images upon the energy.

We have a constant stream of energy that flows from our spiritual selves into our lower beings. Before we forgot that we are spiritual beings, we would impose mental images upon this energy and these images would be based on the individuality anchored in our spiritual self. This would cause the energies to take on forms that helped raise all life. As a result, the energy we were sending out into this world would be based on love and it would create an upward spiral. Our spiritual selves would then give us more energy to drive our further co-creation, and we would actually receive more energy than we had used. Thus, our co-creative powers would be increased.

After we forgot that we are spiritual beings and came to see ourselves as disconnected, separate beings, the scenario changed. When we express energy through fear instead of love, we receive *less* energy from our spiritual selves. The stream of creative energy can eventually be reduced until it is barely enough to keep our physical bodies alive and our minds conscious.

What happens to the energy that we project out through fear? Part of it is sent out into the material realm, where it eventually cycles back to us as what spiritual teachings call karma. Some of the energy becomes stored in our lower beings, what we normally call the subconscious mind. The ascended masters teach that there are four levels of the mind:

- *The identity level.* This is where we find our deepest sense of who (or what) we think we are. Do we see ourselves as spiritual beings who are connected to a higher source with unlimited creative power? Do we see ourselves as human beings who are limited to what we can do with our physical bodies?

- *The mental level.* This is where we find our thoughts, including our sense of how to do things. An important point to understand is that the four levels of the mind form a hierarchical structure. The mental level is below the identity level, so thoughts cannot override your sense of identity. If you see yourself solely as a human being, your thoughts will not be able to question that sense of identity—at least not in a way that will be believable to you. Your sense of identity sets impenetrable boundaries for your thoughts.

• *The emotional level.* This is obviously where you find feelings. The source of feelings is your thoughts, and the source of your thoughts is your sense of identity. If you see yourself as a human being, you will think your life is bound by certain limitations and this will give rise to feelings of fear, powerlessness and anger. You might think such feelings are unavoidable or justifiable.

• *The physical level.* This is the level of the mind that deals with the physical body. A part of this "body computer" needs to be subconscious because it directs the mechanical functions of the body, such as the beating of your heart and many other mechanisms. For many people the physical body eats up the majority of their conscious attention. They are very focused on the needs of the body, including protection, food and sex.

Changing the energy equation

The important lesson here is that when you go into a lower emotional reaction, such as fear, you are coloring or misqualifying creative energy with a specific matrix. Some of that energy will accumulate in the four levels of the mind. Once the accumulation reaches a critical mass, it will exert a magnetic pull on your conscious attention—and your attention will be pulled into certain repetitive patterns. You have no doubt met people who easily get angry and who take a long time to get over their anger. We have incarnated many times on this turbulent planet, which means we have most likely accumulated a lot of energy at the four levels of the mind.

It is no wonder that our conscious attention has been magnetized by this energy and is now focused on the physical body, our emotions or the intellect. You probably know some people whose attention is focused on the body, others who live in their emotions and still others who are intellectually inclined. It depends on which of those areas—the body, mind or emotions—has the highest concentration of psychic energy.

A necessary ingredient for spiritual growth is to let go of the illusions of the human self. I also said that it can be very painful when one of these illusions is exposed. We can now see what causes the pain, namely the misqualified energy accumulated at the four levels of the mind.

I have many times experienced how I started seeing an illusion in my own psyche and this caused a very intense outburst of emotional pain. When I was new to the spiritual path, this used to scare me. I have seen people give up on therapy or even a spiritual practice because they were so scared by the intensity of the energies they encountered in their own minds. This is especially true for people who had a difficult or abusive childhood. I personally had an easy childhood, but I still used to fear that maybe I would one day uncover something so painful that I wouldn't be able to deal with it.

In some cases, this can be a necessary defense mechanism. If there is so much accumulated energy that we cannot handle it, it might be necessary to keep the lid on it for a while longer. Yet at what point do our defense mechanisms become the main block to our progress by causing us to always submit to the human self and its unwillingness to change?

We need to find a balance between wanting freedom from illusion and the pain of taking a look into the depths of the psyche. When I was new to the spiritual path I feared that my ego could be exposed and cause me a major embarrassment. At the same time, I had a clear sense that even if exposing an illusion caused me pain, overcoming the illusion would lead to greater peace of mind. Avoiding a temporary pain was never as important to me as attaining long-term freedom. The equation is straightforward:

- You will never find self-esteem until you get back to a pure sense of self.

- What blocks the pure sense of self is the human self. You are still the pure self, but you are perceiving the world (and yourself) through the filter of the human self.

- The key to your freedom is to dissolve the illusions of the human self. This can only be done by consciously seeing the illusions and then replacing them with higher knowledge.

- In order to come to see an illusion, you must look into the psyche.

- Whenever you look into the psyche, you will contact the misqualified energies stored there, and this will cause you either emotional pain, mental anguish or even an existential fear.

We now see a potentially very liberating conclusion. One of the main factors that blocks self-esteem and makes our lives miserable is the misqualified energy that is stored at the four levels of our minds.

If the accumulation of energy is above a critical mass, it can block us from making any kind of spiritual progress. Our lives will become centered around avoiding looking into the psyche. This will only add to the amount of energy stored in the subconscious and this will make our lives even more miserable. Overcoming such self-reinforcing spirals is an obvious way to free ourselves from the past.

Making the decision to change

I have met people who were trapped in a downward spiral until it got so bad that they finally opened up their minds to a different approach to the problem. For Jill this opening of the mind did not come until she was close to suicide. By actually contemplating taking her own life, she realized that if she had the power to end her life, she should also have the power to change it.

George had a nervous breakdown and became aware that now that he had done the most embarrassing thing he could imagine, he was still alive and that meant the embarrassment existed only in his own mind. Once he faced what he feared and lived through it, his life was no longer controlled by the fear.

Hank grew up with an alcoholic father and also got into substance abuse. One day he noticed that he had gone even lower than his father and he simply could not imagine that he could go any lower. By feeling that he had hit rock bottom, he suddenly saw that there was no longer anything to prove by going down and he felt free to start going up. It is a fact that a substantial portion of the people I have met turned to spirituality as a result of going through a major crisis, which finally caused them to rethink their lives.

I have also met many people on the spiritual path who never had to go that far, because something else opened their minds to the need to change the equation. Ralph, for example, told me that by observing his father's temper tantrums and enduring occasional beatings, he understood that there had to be an explanation for why his father sometimes seemed to be a different person, almost as if he had been possessed. Spiritual teachings helped him see that his father was indeed possessed and had also taught him how to protect himself from the influence of lower forces.

Changing the equation of your life is relatively simple. The cause of the problem is an accumulation of misqualified energy. This energy was generated by your mind. It was generated because your mind has a very fundamental ability. This is an ability that you were never taught about as you grew up, but it is completely natural. What is this mystical ability? It is the ability to change the vibration of psychic energy.

For example, look at what actually happens when we become angry. An angry person is putting out a lot of energy. Where does that energy come from? It comes from the person's higher self. As the energy streams through the four levels of the person's mind, it is gradually lowered in vibration. The identity mind may give it a vibration of being powerless and frustrated. The mental mind might give it a vibration of being a victim. And the emotional mind then gives it a vibration of anger, which is expressed at the physical level.

Why is your mind able to do this? Because the mind has a built-in ability to change the vibration of energy, to qualify or misqualify energy. Doesn't it, then, seem logical that if the mind has the ability to lower the vibration of energy, the mind also has the ability to raise the vibration of energy? In other words, the mind can raise the vibration of the misqualified energy that has accumulated at the four levels of the mind.

What if you could learn to make conscious use of this ability and thereby reduce the amount of misqualified energy accumulated in, for example, your emotional mind? Imagine that you could look into your own psyche without being overwhelmed by intense emotional energy. This is simply a matter of reducing the amount of energy that has accumulated in the subconscious mind. Imagine how much easier it would be to see the illusions of the human self and how this might help you break old patterns of behavior, painful emotions and obsessive thoughts. Imagine how it could help you discover a true and lasting form of self-esteem.

Do you know people who are very sincere in trying to change but who nevertheless are pulled back into old self-destructive patterns? A big factor in this yo-yo approach to personal growth is that these people have not learned to purify their energy fields from lower energies. Thus, the accumulated energies form a magnetic pull that forces their conscious minds back into the old patterns.

Changing your energy field

I still remember what a major breakthrough it was for me to not only understand this but to actually experience that I could free myself from misqualified energies. One day I was practicing a technique for invoking a form of spiritual energy called the violet flame. I was reminded of a situation that happened in high school when I made a fool of myself in front of a girl I had a crush on at the time. This situation would come to my mind once in a while and it usually caused me to feel the same intense emotional pain as when the situation happened. On this particular day I noticed I no longer felt the pain. The only change I had made in my life was that for several months I had practiced this technique for invoking spiritual light. The only explanation I could see was that the light I invoked had transformed the misqualified energies so I could now think about the situation without feeling the emotional pain that had so far made this unbearable. It suddenly hit me: "This stuff really works!"

The technique I had been practicing was given by the ascended masters, and it teaches us how to use our voice, the spoken word, to invoke high-frequency spiritual energy of a certain vibration. As science tells us, when two waves meet, they form an interference pattern that transforms both waves. So by directing a wave of high-frequency energy into the low-frequency energy in our subconscious minds, we can raise the vibration of the lower energy.

This is a purely mechanical interaction—the trick is to find a way to invoke high-frequency energy. Fortunately, our minds have a built-in ability to do this. There is more than one way to open up a flow of high-frequency energy into your mind. There is a natural stream of such energy coming from your spiritual self. I have met people who are able to go into deep meditation or go into their hearts, and this opens up a stream of love from their spiritual selves. They can then consciously direct this love energy into transforming lower energies in both their own minds or the minds of other people.

When I was young I simply wasn't able to do this. There was so much static in my mind that I could not go into my heart and feel the love from my I AM Presence, let alone direct this love. Therefore, I needed something more practical, and what I found was a technique called decrees. These decrees use short affirmations that you say out loud with great power. When you say the words with a certain speed, they have a rhythm, and from the very beginning I could feel how this opened up a flow of energy from the spiritual realm.

In the beginning, I was very shy about saying words out loud because I had been used to meditating in silence. After I got over my initial hesitation, I immediately felt the energy I invoked. Within three months of using decrees, I had experienced three very dramatic effects. One was that I felt my anxiety level drop dramatically and I began to feel less noise in the emotional and mental levels of my mind. I also started going to sleep within 15 minutes instead of tossing and turning for two hours. And I was able to deal with painful situations from the past.

I still use decrees and other techniques for invoking light today, nearly 30 years later. I like to say that if I haven't personally experienced something that is available in the spiritual marketplace, I know someone who has. I think that if there had been a more efficient technique for transforming lower psychic energy, I would have found it. I believe that people who are ready for a change could have amazing benefits from invoking spiritual light.

Over the last 10 years, I have brought forth a lot of decrees and invocations from the ascended masters. You can find them for free along with instructions on how to use them on my

website: *transcendencetoolbox.com*. Regardless of which technique you prefer to use, I consider it essential for all spiritual
seekers to become aware of misqualified energy, how it accu-
mulates and how to free yourself from its influence. Based on
my experience, I simply can't see how you can make serious
progress on the spiritual path without being aware of energy
and doing something about it. What I have learned from the
ascended masters is that I need to do three things with energy:

- I need to create a shield of spiritual energy around
my personal energy field so that I am protected from
the lower energies in the mass consciousness.

- I need to use spiritual energy to cut myself free
from any ties to the mass consciousness.

- I need to use spiritual energy to transform the misqualified energies that are already inside my energy field.

These principles have been important to me because they
give us a very practical way to approach spiritual growth as a
systematic, gradual path. Some spiritual teachers say there is
nothing you can do to become enlightened and that you simply need to wait for a spontaneous awakening experience. The
way I see it is that enlightenment is the natural state of the pure
self. We are not currently enlightened because the pure self has
been pulled into the human self, and thus we look at the world
through the filter of that self.

In order to get back to the pure state, we can't simply sit
around and wait for this to happen spontaneously—because
it won't. The reason is that we have free will and we created
the human self by making certain choices. The only way to

get back to a pure state is to consciously undo those choices and shed the illusions that make up the superstructure of the human self.

But those decisions are covered behind a pile of misqual-ified energy at the emotional, mental and identity levels of the subconscious mind. This energy is purely mechanical, and transforming it is also a somewhat mechanical process. If you have X amount of accumulated energy, you need to invoke X amount of spiritual energy to transform it.

This does not mean that when all of the energy is trans-formed, we will automatically become enlightened, as I thought when I was younger and as many people seem to think. We still have to consciously undo the choices we made in the past, for example the choice to accept ourselves as limited, mortal human beings.

Yet once the energy is gone, it becomes so much easier to clearly see our past choices and how they limit us. Once we see that a decision is hurting us, we will almost spontaneously let go of that decision and make a better choice.

The dangers of the doing phase

When we first find the spiritual path, we can go through an experimental phase where we sample what is available in the marketplace. During this phase, we often believe there is a quick and easy way to become enlightened. It is a necessary loss to have this illusion collapse, but for some people it can be very painful. I have met people who gave up on all forms of spirituality after having this illusion come tumbling down. You now know what causes this pain, and thus you can do something about it.

Most people I have met are able to handle this loss and they often do so by adopting a much more serious approach to spiritual growth. They accept that it requires both study and sustained practice, which then leads them into the "doing phase." They find a spiritual teacher who promotes a particular form of spiritual practice and they now decide to apply it very diligently. I myself have spent thousands of hours doing decrees and I know people who have been very diligent in other forms of spiritual practice.

I am in no way saying there is anything wrong with going into the doing phase. Whatever technique people are using, they are attempting to decrease the static in their energy fields and this is an absolutely necessary part of spiritual growth. We need to do something to reduce the amount of low-frequency energy so we can get a clearer signal from our spiritual selves.

In the beginning, I thought the doing phase was not a phase but that it would lead me to the end goal of my path. I thought that if I continued to practice decrees long enough and hard enough, I would one day wake up and be enlightened. After a few years I saw that it is only a step on the path. I am not saying that we will or should ever stop using some form of spiritual practice. I am saying that there comes a point for most people where they realize that doing something is not an end in itself. In other words, we need to consciously undo our past choices, and performing a spiritual practice will not automatically accomplish this.

In terms of self-esteem, there is a real risk that the doing phase can cause us to develop so much me-esteem and we-esteem that we find it hard to let go of this and move on. When I first heard about ascended masters, I found an American movement that was very focused on giving decrees. This movement would arrange conferences and weekly meetings where people would decree as a group for the improvement of various world conditions.

It was a very powerful experience for me to have three thousand people decreeing together in a big circus tent for a summer conference. I could literally feel how the number of people increased the power of the decrees. After a four-hour decree service, I felt that my consciousness had been lifted far beyond its normal level. In the beginning, I threw myself into this work with all my youthful enthusiasm, and as a result I developed a strong sense of we-esteem for being part of this advanced group of spiritual students. We believed that we had the most advanced spiritual teaching on the planet and that our decrees were helping open the way for a golden age.

I also spent many hours decreeing on my own, and I developed a strong sense of me-esteem for being so dedicated to this practice. Eventually a question came to my mind: "How much do I have to do in order to feel I have compensated for my lack of self-esteem?" The equation is simple: The lower your self-esteem, the more you will think you have to do. This can lead us into an unbalanced approach where we put so much focus on our spiritual practice that we neglect other aspects of life. I personally went through a period where I spent so much time with my spiritual practice that I felt I could not allow myself to enjoy life, and I have seen many other people do the same.

The question now becomes how unbalanced we have to become—how severe of a crisis we have to experience—before we realize we need to look for a more balanced approach. After spending several years being focused on saving the world, it gradually started dawning on me that decreeing so much had become an excuse for not looking into my personal psychological hang-ups. I then knew it was time for me to move into the next phase of my personal path. Had I not been able to do this, I could have become stuck in the doing phase, and although it gave me both me-esteem and we-esteem, it never would have taken me to true self-esteem.

Keys from Chapter 3

◊ **The human self** wants us to believe we can make spiritual progress and achieve self-esteem without resolving conflict in our psyches. This can lead spiritual students to look for a quick-fix. Eventually, most people realize spiritual growth is a lifetime commitment that requires work.

◊ **The spiritual path** can be seen as a spiral staircase with many steps. Many people have found a spiritual teacher or movement that corresponded to a certain step. The trick is to avoid getting stuck so you can recognize when it is time to find a teacher who can take you higher.

◊ **What keeps you at a certain level of your path** is the illusions you have accepted and the energies you have colored or misqualified through those illusions.

◊ **We have the co-creative abilities** to work with the basic form of energy that makes up the material universe. Our minds can form mental images and project them onto the basic creative energy, causing it to take on form.

◊ **We have a spiritual self** that contains the blueprint of our true individuality. This cannot be destroyed by anything we have experienced in the material world.

◊ **The pure self** descended as an extension of the spiritual self in order to co-create in the material world.

◊   **The pure self** created a human self and eventually became so blinded by it that it forgot its connection to the I AM Presence. The purpose of the spiritual path is to restore this connection. This is done by dissolving the illusions and energies that make up the human self.

◊   **An essential step on the spiritual path** is to learn how to use spiritual techniques to purify the energies generated through the human self. These misqualified energies form a magnetic pull on our attention that keeps us trapped in thinking we are human beings.

4 | HEALING YOUR INNER WOUNDS

There are two factors that block our growth by keeping us trapped in the human self. One is a belief about ourselves and life that we have decided to accept. The other is the energy we have colored or misqualified through this belief and that has now accumulated in the four levels of our minds. The doing phase of our spiritual path reduces the accumulated energy, but if we do not resolve the belief, we will continue to misqualify energy through it. We can enter a kind of treadmill where we use a spiritual practice to transform the energy, but at the same time we are generating more low-frequency energy. The net gain is either nonexistent or much smaller than it could be. You may be using a spiritual practice to take two steps forward, but the unresolved belief causes you to slide one step backward.

I spent about five years being very focused on my spiritual practice, spending at least a couple of hours a day invoking spiritual light. I have no doubt that during those years I was making genuine progress; I was purifying more energy than I was misqualifying through my unresolved beliefs. I was reducing the amount of chaos or static in the four levels of my mind, which caused me to improve my intuition and get a better feel for my divine plan. Yet I was not making progress as fast as I could have done and this gradually became clear to me. I became aware that I was dragging a dead weight behind me and I knew it was time for me to do something about it.

This breakthrough could have come sooner if I had known what I know today. Instead, my progress was held back by two mechanisms that I have seen in action in many spiritual seekers.

The desire to save the world

Most spiritual people have a strong sense that they are here on earth to fulfill a mission that reaches beyond themselves. Many spiritual movements address this by giving people the feeling that by being a member of the organization and performing its practices, you are indeed making an important contribution to bringing about positive change on this planet. I think this claim is entirely correct.

It has been obvious to me from a young age that all human beings are connected in consciousness through what Carl Jung called the "collective unconscious." It is equally clear that the conditions—should we say the train wreck?—we currently see on this planet is a reflection of the collective consciousness of its people. This leads to what is, for me, an important conclusion, namely that the only way to improve conditions on this planet is to raise the collective consciousness. How do we do this? Well, I do believe that spiritual practices, such as meditation or invoking light through decrees, prayers, affirmations and other techniques, can transform the misqualified energy that has accumulated in the collective energy field. However, the real way to raise the collective is for enough people to raise their consciousness on an individual basis. The collective consciousness is made up of our individual minds, so if you raise your mind, you will help pull up the whole.

There are many ways to raise awareness and they generally center around studying spiritual teachings, performing spiritual practices and applying a spiritual outlook in all aspects of our lives. What we have seen on a worldwide scale since the 1960s is that millions of individuals have attempted to raise their consciousness through spiritual practices. In recorded history, this has never before been seen on such a scale and I believe it is gradually transforming the world.

I also see that while performing a spiritual practice is an important contribution, it is not the ultimate contribution. If we really want to help raise the planet, we must raise our consciousness to the level where we have transcended the human self and returned to the pure self. We must reach a state of consciousness that is distinctly higher than what our nonspiritual society calls "normal" human awareness.

The question now becomes whether we can raise our consciousness exclusively by performing a spiritual practice. Can the legitimate desire to help change the world become a diversion that causes us to focus our attention on changing other people instead of changing ourselves?

No mechanical way to spiritual growth

Many spiritual teachings talk about a higher state of consciousness by using various names and descriptions. I believe there are many millions of people today who have the potential to reach a higher state of consciousness in this lifetime. At an early stage, I sensed that I am one of them. Ever since then, reaching a higher state of consciousness has been the overall goal for my involvement with spiritual teachings and movements.

When I was new to the spiritual path, I was susceptible to an idea that is not really taught by spiritual teachers but that is nevertheless floating around in the collective consciousness. I believe this idea is partly created by the fact that we have grown up in a society so dominated by technology. The thing about technology is that it works in a mechanical way. If you go into a dark room and flip a switch on the wall, you expect that this will make the light come on. If you get into your car and turn the key, you expect the engine to start. You have two ingredients in the technological mindset—an expectation of a result and an action you need to take in order to trigger the result. Even beyond that is the expectation that when you do perform the trigger action, the result will follow automatically. If the result does not follow, then something has gone wrong somewhere.

Now consider what has happened since the 1960s. Millions of people who have grown up in a technological society have been experimenting with spiritual teachings. Because we don't have a well-known spiritual tradition in the West, many have turned to Eastern gurus. I am not sure an Indian guru necessarily understands that when he talks about meditation leading to a higher state of consciousness, many Westerners will view meditation as a piece of technology. They expect that if they perform the meditation, then a higher state of consciousness should follow automatically. If it doesn't, they will feel something has gone wrong and then they will blame the guru.

I have been a member of two spiritual movements that promoted different spiritual practices and in each movement some people expected that by performing the practice as prescribed, they would automatically reach a higher state of consciousness. I have met people who have experienced the same mechanism in other spiritual movements, and you can find discussion forums on the internet that make it clear this is a general trend. It took me many years to understand what really should have been obvious to me from the beginning— that *reaching a higher state of consciousness is not a mechanical process.*

It is true that the process has certain mechanical elements. I have already described that one of the main factors that blocks our spiritual progress is misqualified energy that has accumulated in the four levels of our minds. Invoking light of a higher frequency to raise the vibration of this energy is a fairly mechanical process. If you invoke a certain amount of spiritual light, you will transform a certain amount of lower energy.

I have also attempted to make it clear that this lower energy is generated by us. It is generated when pure energy from our spiritual selves passes through a limited or dysfunctional belief in our subconscious minds. The lower energy is only the effect; the cause is the belief and it is based on a decision. Until we actually overcome the decision to accept a limited self-image, we will not take a step towards returning to a pure sense of self.

There is only one way to overcome a decision made in the past and that is to take a look at it in the present, see it as a limiting decision and then consciously replace it by making a better decision.

I used to think there had to be a shortcut that could circumvent this process of consciously looking at myself. I eventually understood that this is precisely the problem with mainstream religion. Most mainstream religions make the promise that if you are a member, if you follow all the outer rules and if you believe in all the outer doctrines, you will automatically be saved. The most obvious version of this is the fundamentalist churches who claim that if you declare Jesus to be your Lord and Savior, he simply has to save you no matter what you have done.

I'll never forget how during a visit to a good friend in California I met Gill, whose father was an evangelical minister with his own television station. During our discussion, Gill used the standard fundamentalist rhetoric in an attempt to refute what he saw as my New Age beliefs. I suddenly blurted out: "So if Hitler on his deathbed had confessed Christ, would Hitler have gone to heaven?" I could literally feel how this question created instant inner turmoil in Gill. He finally answered that according to everything he had been brought up to believe in, he would have to say that if Hitler had been sincere, he would have been saved. But I could tell Gill knew that something didn't quite add up.

What in my view doesn't add up is that Jesus didn't teach an automatic path to salvation. This is so clear from many statements he made, but especially from the appeal that we stop looking at the splinter in the eyes of other people and look at the beam in our own eyes. My point here is not to focus on the flaws of fundamentalist Christians but to use these beliefs as an example that I know many spiritual people can see as illogical.

We can then turn to the mirror ourselves and see how we may have adopted the exact same mindset, though in a more subtle way.

I freely admit that when I was young I was indeed affected by the belief that by following a spiritual teaching and doing thousands of hours of decrees I would automatically make my ascension, reach a higher state of consciousness and fulfill my life plan. After several years, I started noticing that the ascended masters actually never presented the ascension as an automatic process. Instead, they did talk a lot about the necessity of resolving our psychological wounds and hang-ups.

I had indeed made progress by spending thousands of hours praying and decreeing for the world. Doing this had also transformed some of the accumulated energy in my own mind. Therefore, it had been perfectly right for me to adopt this lifestyle—for a time. However, one day I was watching a television program on the second world war, and I realized a soldier at war has to go into a very distinct mindset. He has to be so focused on physical survival that there is no room in his mind for the "touchy-feely" stuff of working on his psychology.

I suddenly had a breakthrough experience where I saw that I had adopted the same mindset as if I was at war. I then understood that no one can live this way for too long without getting battle fatigue. If I had been a solider who had participated in the second world war, I would have been in this mindset for a maximum of five years. I had now been living my own unbalanced lifestyle for about that amount of time. When I saw this, I instantly recognized it was time for a change.

I saw that I had been using the valid goal of improving the world as an excuse for not looking at my own psychology. While this had been constructive for a time, it simply could not take me to my ultimate goal of reaching a higher state of consciousness.

"I don't have psychological problems"

I had been aware of the need to work on my psychology for a couple of years, but I kept postponing it. The main reason was that I did not consider myself to be the kind of person who would need therapy. Part of the reason was that when I grew up, the only people who ever entered a psychologist's office arrived in a straightjacket.

I had a quite normal and harmonious upbringing, and I had met many people on the path who were spiritual seekers precisely because their upbringing had given them such trauma that they could clearly see the need for healing. I know this will seem crazy, but it can actually be an advantage to have had such difficulties in childhood that the need for healing is obvious. Because I was so "normal," I felt no need for healing and this gave my human self the perfect excuse.

If you look at humanity as a whole, you can see that we human beings have an amazing ability to adapt to a variety of circumstances. I have been fascinated by reading about people who experienced losing everything during war; some went into a state of psychic paralysis, whereas others were able to move on. Why were some people able to move on after severe trauma? Because the human self is very good at establishing a new "normal state."

When we experience trauma, the human self immediately splits into two selves. One will feel the full force of the trauma and be paralyzed and the other will deny the trauma. If the traumatized self wins, people are paralyzed and cannot move on. If the denying self wins, it can manage to suppress the feeling of trauma at the level of conscious awareness. The advantage of that is that people can respond to the situation in a better way, but the long-term cost is that the traumatized self still remains in the subconscious. The one thing you can rely on is that whatever is hidden in the subconscious mind will eventually surface. In fact, for you to return to your pure self, everything subconscious must become conscious and be dismissed.

As I said, I moved to the United States in 1987 and had several very turbulent years. I was able to deal with this and move on, but I knew I had suppressed many feelings. In the early 1990s, I acknowledged that I simply had to deal with these feelings if I wanted to reach a higher state of consciousness. I also started having intuitive flashes of having been killed in past lifetimes, which is highly likely when you consider the history of this planet. Even if I had not been traumatized in this lifetime, it had most certainly happened in past lifetimes and I was carrying the wounds in my subconscious mind.

I eventually came to the conclusion that I wanted to fulfill my divine plan and that I did not want to have anything stand in the way of that goal—including my personal psychology. This determination caused me to take a step that my family might have considered worse than entering a spiritual movement: I entered therapy.

I had experimented with inner child workshops but really didn't feel it had given me what I needed. I was then fortunate to find a therapist who had a traditional education as a clinical psychologist and also a spiritual outlook. I did weekly sessions with her, and she used a combination of talk therapy, gestalt and a technique called EMDR (Eye Movement Desensitization and Reprocessing). This continued for a period of six months, until we both felt I had reached a breakthrough and it was time for me to take a break.

The therapy was a major step forward for me, especially because it helped me overcome some wounds that had haunted me since childhood. I clearly see that the wounds originated in a past lifetime, but they had been reinforced because of my relationship with my father. One of the most powerful experiences during therapy was to do a gestalt session where I first said everything I had never said to my father. Then I changed chairs and now said what I felt he would have said in response. It was a major release and I really felt as if a heavy weight had been lifted from me.

Do we all need therapy?

In my personal case, therapy really worked. I have learned, however, that it is dangerous to make generalizations—generally speaking. I am not saying everyone needs a particular form of therapy, but in a sense life gives all of us therapy. In its broadest form, therapy is when we get someone who is outside our personal mental box to give us feedback on what is happening in our psyches—which we cannot see from inside the box.

This outside feedback is absolutely necessary, because the very nature of the human self is that it does form a closed mental box. As I mentioned, the second law of thermodynamics will make sure that any closed system breaks down. You may not have had what is normally called a breakdown, but you may experience a period of very little growth. I have personally seen many people who did everything right according to a spiritual teaching but who simply were not transcending themselves. Ruth, for example, had been following ascended master teachings for more than 30 years when I met her. She had spent thousands of hours invoking the violet flame energy to transform lower energies. She had studied the teachings in great depth and had a good intellectual understanding of the path to the ascension. Unfortunately, she had not actually connected the outer teaching to her personal life and her psychological wounds from childhood. Even though she was a very kind person, she did not change at all during the 10 years I knew her.

In my view, she had used a spiritual teaching to create an even more closed mental box than she had before finding that teaching. By observing Ruth I understood that I had done the same thing to some degree, and when I saw it, I decided to make a change.

The most powerful aspect of having our mental box exposed is that it can give us a true breakthrough experience. While reading a book, I have many times had an aha experience where I felt "Aha, now I understand this." But it is far more powerful when you have an experience that involves all four aspects of your mind. You suddenly feel like you are much more conscious and aware. You feel a release of emotional energy or tension. You see a situation or your psychology with great clarity, and all this shifts your sense of self at the identity level.

I imagine you have already had such experiences during your spiritual search. If not, you can help bring them about by invoking spiritual light to minimize the static in the physical, emotional and mental minds. Once you have done that, you can benefit greatly from developing a habit that most spiritual seekers develop, often without actually realizing it. This is the habit of self-observation. Here we have another example of the need for a delicate balance.

When you have been deeply hurt, you often go into a frame of mind of being very focused on yourself. I have always had a habit of analyzing myself and my behavior, often going over situations again and again—as if dwelling on the past could somehow change what happened. That is not actually self-observation; it is obsessive-compulsive behavior and it comes from the human self.

It comes from the fact that there is one part of the human self that is constantly feeling the pain from the past and there is another part that is seeking to cover over the pain. The constant tension between them causes you to focus on yourself, because you constantly have to be on guard for situations that might trigger the pain. You are, in essence, spending all your attention on either seeking to avoid having the pain flare up or doing damage control after it has happened. It is not a pleasant way to live.

When I talk about self-observation, I mean a deeper mechanism that has one all-important characteristic: It is nonjudgmental. I imagine you have noticed that it is always easy to see what other people should have done. The reason is that you are not looking at their situation from inside their mental box. You are looking from the outside in, and thus you are detached from their emotions and illusions. You can look at the situation calmly and thus the solution is obvious.

I am sure you have also experienced that when it comes to your own situation, you are very much affected by a limited vision and a strong emotional pull. Now think back to situations you experienced during childhood. I imagine you have some situations that you can look at with no emotional tension. The reason is that these situations either did not create a psychological wound or you have healed the wound so you now feel the situation is no big deal. Wouldn't it be wonderful to be able to look at everything from your past with such peace? Well, it is possible, but only when you heal the psychological wounds. Doing this can seem like one of the hardest things we human beings can do. Nevertheless, it is a skill we can learn, just like learning to walk.

How do we learn it? We can begin by thinking about a baby who is learning to walk. The baby is constantly trying to get up, and when it falls down, it simply tries again. Now imagine that you took a baby and every time it fell down, you scolded it severely and called it stupid. There is a real risk that such a child either would not learn to walk or would grow up with a severe emotional trauma that could be triggered by the slightest stumble.

Why don't you have such a wound related to walking? Because no one scolded you for falling down. Why do you have other wounds? Because someone did scold you for failing or for not being perfect.

Let's now return to what I have said about the human self, namely that it always has two polarities. You have certain wounds because in the past—perhaps in a past lifetime that is now forgotten—you experienced a severe trauma. That created two aspects of the human self, one that is blaming you for what you did and one that is seeking to cover it over or compensate for it. This has now become your new normal state, and as long as a certain equilibrium is maintained, you can keep a relative peace—you can live with this.

That's like walking on eggshells, though, and the slightest provocation can plunge you into pain. The problem is that when you have such wounds, you will want to maintain your normal state, which means you do not want to look into the psyche. In fact, part of your human self says this is dangerous and must be avoided at all costs. What can break the stalemate?

The key for me has been to understand two things. One is that the human self always has (at least) two opposing aspects, which creates constant tension. The other is to realize that my pure self is still pure. I have two human selves fighting each other and I have created those selves, but I have not become those selves. I am still the pure self; I am simply experiencing the world through the filter of the human selves.

At any moment, my pure self can become aware of itself as being pure, as being more than the human selves. That experience is what I call pure self-observation. This state of mind is mentioned by every spiritual and mystical tradition. Jesus told us we have to become as little children. Zen Buddhists talk about beginner's mind. Other mystical traditions call it silent witnessing, gnosis or naked awareness. Eckhart Tolle has written and lectured extensively on this shift and gives a very good description of it in his book *The Power of Now*.

You may not have experienced this state of mind or you may not have been consciously aware of having the experience, but you can start right now. Simply close your eyes and become aware that you are sitting here reading this book. Before I asked you to do this, your awareness was probably fully invested in reading. By doing this simple exercise, you are now aware that you are reading the book, almost as if you are observing yourself from the outside. What is the self that is aware that you are reading this book? Is there more than one self in your mind?

There *is* more than one self, because the human self can never step outside itself—it can never actually become self-aware. Only the pure self can disidentify itself from what you are doing, step outside of the body and of the human self and look at them from the outside. This simple act of self-observation is the essential key to reclaiming your true sense of self and thereby setting a foundation for lasting self-esteem.

The magic of this self-observation is that the pure self is pure, meaning it has no judgments. Value judgments, and the pain springing from them, come from the two aspects of the human self fighting against each other. The pure self simply sees a situation, recognizes the ongoing struggle of the human selves and recognizes that the struggle is inconsequential and can never lead to a decisive outcome. Once it sees this, you can make a conscious decision that you no longer want to be trapped on this merry-go-round of the human selves. This can shift your sense of self because you can now choose to leave behind part of the human self. For you to do this, you must come to see and undo the decision that created both aspects of the human self.

How our wounds limit our growth

Consider this in relation to the esteem balance. If seeing an illusion would cause too great of a loss of self-esteem, we refuse to look at the illusion. The same goes for an emotional wound. You can only heal the wound by looking at it, but if looking at it would cause too much pain or loss of esteem, you will refuse to look at it.

This, of course, causes you to remain trapped in the wounded behavior, but that situation is livable because the human self has turned the wound into its new normal. This situation is what I like to call a psychological catch-22. In case you are not familiar with this expression, it is the title of a book by Joseph Heller. He describes a person who was a bomber pilot during the second world war, flying almost suicidal missions over Europe. The pilot wants to get out, but the only chance he has is to be declared too insane to fly. In order to be declared insane, he has to ask for an evaluation from the flight surgeon. Unfortunately, the surgeon is of the opinion that asking for an evaluation proves that you are a rational person. And if you are a rational person, you cannot be too insane to fly.

Take note of the irony and how this relates to what I said about the human self's ability to establish a new normal. Clearly, flying these combat missions, where you could be shot or burned to death or you might kill innocent civilians, was an act of insanity. But the war had caused flying these missions to be considered the new normal. Because the norm was clearly insane behavior, only crazy people would actually fly. The only way to get out of flying was to prove that you were crazy. But the very desire to get out of a form of insanity proved you were a rational person, and in that state you could not be declared too crazy to fly.

That is a good example of how the human self is able to trick us into doing something that is either unbalanced or causes us constant tension. But we think it cannot be any other way and thus we accept it as normal. How can we snap out of this illusion, acknowledge we have a problem and decide to do something about it? There are basically two ways.

In her well-known book *A Return to Love*, Marianne Williamson describes how she had several very turbulent years in her youth, but she was not able to break free from her patterns. In the language I am using here, I would say the explanation was that two aspects of her human self caused her unbalanced behavior, but because she had come to see them as part of her normal state, she could not break free. She describes how she had a nervous breakdown and finally said: "God, help me."

In her words, she sees this as an act of surrender to a higher power in recognition of the fact that she could not free herself. She calls this a state of humility, but one might also call it an act of self-observation—the kind only the pure self can experience. Her pure self had begun to separate itself from the divisions of the human self, and she had started to see that *the human self cannot set you free from the problems created by the human self.*

Many spiritual people do not have to experience a breakdown in order to become open to a better approach. Many are able to use a spiritual teaching to arrive at the following realization:

- My positive goal is that I want to attain a higher state of consciousness.

- What blocks my growth is that there is something in my subconscious mind that I have not seen.

- I have the determination to reach a higher state of consciousness, and I will not let my psychological hang-ups sabotage my goal. Thus, I am willing to take a look at myself.

- It may cause me pain to look at my wounds, but I am deciding that I am willing to endure this temporary pain in order to be free in the long run.

The effect of shifting into this willingness to look at yourself is that you now fulfill the basic requirement for spiritual progress, namely that you are open to a teacher who can help you see the hidden aspects of your human self. And as I have mentioned a time or two, when the student is ready, the …

Finding your inner teacher

During my six months of therapy, I worked on issues ranging from my childhood to much deeper issues. Once the more surface wounds had been transcended, I could look at some of the deeper, existential wounds. In my last session, I worked on the sense of being abandoned by God. The material world is much denser than the spiritual realm, and when the pure self enters into the human self and a physical body, it is almost inevitable that it loses its conscious awareness of its spiritual self. This has for all of us caused a sense of being abandoned, and we often see it as being abandoned by God.

The reality of the situation is that we have not been abandoned. We only think we have been abandoned because we are perceiving life through the filter of the human self. Through this filter, we simply cannot experience our spiritual selves. The pure self actually has the ability to step outside this perception filter and connect to the I AM Presence. If we have too much accumulated energy and too many limiting beliefs and wounds in the four levels of our minds, it is very difficult for us to do this.

You might compare this to how people sit at night and watch television. We have the physical ability to get up, walk outside, look up into the night sky and experience a sense of wonder and connection to something greater than ourselves. Yet how many people pull themselves away from the television and do this?

The ascended masters know how difficult it is for us to pull ourselves away from the human self and reconnect to the spiritual self. The spiritual self simply cannot lower itself to our present level because its function is to preserve our divine individuality from being destroyed by anything on earth. This will seem like another catch-22. We can't reach up and the spiritual self can't reach down.

What breaks the stalemate is that the ascended masters have used part of their own attainment to create "mediators" that can reach down to where we are in consciousness. They call this our "Christ self." This does not mean the ascended masters want us to become "good Christians." The term *Christ* is actually universal because Jesus' life was an illustration of the Christ principle, which is that something descends from above in order to awaken us to our true potential. Jesus came to serve as an example for the state of consciousness we can all attain.

We all have a Christ self, and it is what most people see as intuition or the "still small voice within." Some call it the higher self. Most spiritual people have had some contact with and guidance from their Christ selves all of their lives. I certainly had this in important moments. Up until my therapy, it had been somewhat sporadic.

What happened at my last session was that I processed a very deep feeling of abandonment and I saw that God had never abandoned me; it was all an illusion created in my human mind. This caused me to accept God and accept myself as a son of God, and when that happened I spontaneously started crying. This wasn't caused by sorrow and not even a release; it was because I experienced the beauty of my I AM Presence. And at that moment I literally felt my Christ self descend upon me and I felt that I bonded with it. This process is what

Jesus referred to in a mystical way as the marriage feast and there are Christian mystics who have talked about being "wed" to Christ. In the well-known book, *A Course in Miracles*, it is said that miracles are a shift in consciousness, what I have called breakthrough experiences. The Course also talks about the anointing, which I see as the process of bonding with your Christ self.

I am describing this experience because it is something I believe we can all have and are meant to have. I believe this is a perfectly natural experience. It is not reserved for superior people and you do not need to have some outer grace or special dispensation. Your Christ self is created to be your personal inner teacher, and it will gladly bond with you, but it will not violate your free will. In order for you to accept your Christ self, you need to clear away some of the misqualified energy and you need to heal some of the wounds that keep you trapped on the treadmill of the human self.

When you have done this, the next step is a conscious recognition and acceptance of your Christ self. Have you ever considered inviting your Christ self to come into your life? If not, you might consider using the decrees and invocations I have mentioned to clear your energy field until you feel a deeper inner connection. You can then consciously, with a simply prayer, invite your Christ self to come into your life and be your personal teacher.

Why is bonding with your inner teacher so important? On a personal level that is the one thing that will speed up your growth more than anything else. Many spiritual people dream of finding a personal guru who can give them constant individual attention. It is not easy to find a good teacher; and if you do, that teacher will most likely attract many students, which means he or she will have limited time for you. Your Christ self is like having your personal guru with you 24 hours a day. It is not as easy to hear your Christ self as it is to hear an outer guru, but as you begin working with your Christ self and continue to transform misqualified energy and heal your wounds, your contact will become clearer.

Looking at this from a more global perspective, we live in an age where humankind has the potential to go through a major spiritual awakening. How will this awakening come about? It will not happen through the traditional Indian model, where a guru sets up an ashram and attracts students he gives personal attention to. Why not? Because there are seven billion people on this planet, and if the collective consciousness is to be raised, it will require that many millions of people raise their consciousness to a higher level. There simply are not enough qualified spiritual teachers to physically tutor so many millions of people. The only realistic solution is that those millions of people develop a bond with their inner teachers, namely their Christ selves and the ascended masters.

Keys from Chapter 4

◊   **The "doing phase" of the spiritual path** is when we are focused on using a spiritual technique to reduce the lower energies in our minds. This is a very necessary phase, but it cannot take us to true self-esteem.

◊   **After we reduce the amount of internal noise,** we can look at the illusions in our subconscious minds. By first reducing the amount of misqualified energy, looking into our illusions can be done with less or no emotional pain.

◊   **It is important to develop the ability to observe yourself** in a neutral way without going into self-condemnation or being overwhelmed by emotional pain.

◊   **We all have an inner teacher** who can and will guide us when we open our minds to acknowledge that guidance. When we transform lower energies and dissolve some illusions, we will naturally begin to see the guidance of our inner teacher. This will help us rise to the next level of the path.

5 | PURIFYING YOUR PERCEPTION FILTER

The fear of having our vulnerabilities exposed is one of the biggest obstacles to our spiritual growth. Until I had the experience of bonding with my inner teacher, I had been trying to make spiritual progress while avoiding and even defending my wounds and illusions. I was scared to look deeply into my psyche, and thus I clung to the belief that by doing outer things I would one day wake up and be enlightened.

Invoking light through my spiritual practice had diminished the energy that had accumulated in the four levels of my mind and this made it far less painful to look at my wounds and illusions. Being in therapy showed me that it is not so terribly hard to expose our illusions and heal our wounds. I simply needed to experience that a sufficient number of times for the sense of danger or mystery to be taken out of it. I came to see that healing my psychology was no harder than so many other things I had learned in this lifetime.

After the experience of bonding with my inner teacher, what I call our Christ self, I went through a major shift. My

Christ self helped me overcome the feeling that God would judge me for having made mistakes. Before this shift, I had an inner fear that if I had a wound because in the past I had made a major mistake, it would be an unbearable shame. In the classical defense mechanism of the human self, I had resisted looking at my wounds. Feeling the presence of my Christ self now made me feel safe because I felt it did not come to judge me but to help me attain freedom from all limitations. And that suddenly made it safe to explore my wounds.

I fully embraced a new approach to the spiritual path, namely that it is an *inner process*. I no longer saw it as an outer path where all I had to do was outer practices. Instead, I saw that the essence of spiritual growth is to overcome my psychological limitations. Instead of running away from dealing with this, I started slowly but surely to embrace the process. I started looking for my wounds instead of seeking to hide from them. I also experienced that although it could be hard to expose a wound and deal with it, each experience made me feel more free, and this put me in an upward spiral that continues to this day.

The highest goal of spiritual growth

From the time I discovered the spiritual path, my goal was to attain a higher state of consciousness. Yet I had a very sketchy view of how to actually accomplish this goal. I did not understand what it takes to attain this higher state of consciousness, nor did I see what it is like. My Christ self helped change this for me.

I was guided to study how the Buddha attained enlightenment. The story goes that Gautama was ready to enter the enlightened state, but he had one last initiation to pass. As he was sitting in meditation under a tree, he was suddenly confronted with Mara, who represents the lord of the material world. Mara conjured up all kinds of demons who paraded before the Buddha by taking on forms that appeared both evil and good.

As I meditated on this, I one day had a breakthrough experience. I saw that what the demons were seeking to do to the Buddha was to force, fool or tempt him into reacting to them. If he had reacted to them in *any* way, he would have demonstrated that he still had an attachment to something on earth and thus he was not ready to enter Nirvana. I understood that the key to Buddhahood is nonattachment to *anything* in the material world and I decided I wanted that state of mind.

What is the key to nonattachment? It is to see how the human self works and then surrender the illusion that gives the human self power over you. As a child I remember being at a country fair and seeing this huge bull being pulled around by a little boy. The bull had a ring in its nose and because the nose is so sensitive, a small boy could drag the bull around by the nose. I understood that my human self has been pulling me around by the nose and I determined that this simply had to stop. I made it my new highest goal to attain nonattachment through seeing and surrendering the illusions of the human self. Naturally, this was easier said than done, but there is a certain magic in having a clear goal and a vision of what it takes to attain it. Once you are willing, it is amazing how your Christ self can guide you to situations or teachings that open your vision.

I understood that the Buddha did not react to the demons because he had purified his mind of all illusions and lower energies. Therefore, there was nothing in his mind that the demons could grab a hold of and use to force him to react. Jesus described this when he said: "The prince of this world cometh and has nothing in me." I decided I wanted to get to that point. I am still striving to get to that point, but I have definitely taken a lot of rings out of my nose.

After contemplating the Buddha for some time, I started realizing that the human self will actively and aggressively seek to stop our spiritual progress. That is why many spiritual teachers and progressive psychologists talk about a human self, or ego, that is like a separate being hiding in our psyches. This being has a survival instinct, and it will seek to influence us in ways that ensure its own survival—regardless of how much suffering this causes us.

How does the human self seek to influence us? One way is by using the psychic energies that have accumulated in the four levels of our minds. The human self can hide behind these energies (they form an energy veil, also called "evil") and it can even direct these energies at our conscious minds. For example, the human self can direct fear energy at our conscious minds, causing us to feel so overwhelmed and confused that we cling to the familiar.

The main weapon that the human self uses to control us is illusions. These can take many forms and they can be very subtle. In many cases, two or more illusions are combined in such a way that from the viewpoint of our conscious minds, there either seems to be no need for change or no way to bring about that change. It seems like we have no way out because the human self has limited our vision so we either do not see the problem or do not see the solution.

It took me many years to see that the human self can survive only by staying hidden from our conscious awareness.

It can hide only because we have accepted certain erroneous beliefs, and thus it will do anything to prevent us from questioning our illusions. Its basic strategy is to divert our attention away from itself. The human self will first seek to make us think certain beliefs are not illusions but instead represent some ultimate reality. When that no longer works, it will seek to make us think looking at our illusions is either unnecessary, too dangerous or simply too complicated.

If you want to take an important step towards exposing your personal human self, simply monitor your reaction as you read on. What kind of energies do you feel in your emotional body? What kind of thoughts come into your mind as you read about the human self? Is there perhaps a prideful sense that you have done so much that you no longer have a human self? Do you have a fear of looking at certain beliefs? Is there a sense of hopelessness that dealing with your psychology is just too complicated and not worth the trouble? Whatever it is for you personally, your human self will seek to present you with a watertight excuse for not accepting what you are reading in this book. Simply observe what happens as you read on.

How the human self uses a spiritual teaching

The human self would have preferred that we had never found the spiritual path because it senses this can be a threat to its control over us. Once it realizes it cannot prevent us from accepting a spiritual teaching, the human self becomes like a chameleon. It will now seek to turn itself into exactly the kind of self that our spiritual teaching describes as the ideal. It will seek to make itself so "spiritual" that we either do not see it or think there is no need to do anything about it. We might even believe we can perfect the human self and that it can one day fool God and find its way into heaven.

Here's an example of how my human self reacted when I found the spiritual path. The human self has at least two divisions. For instance, one part of the human self may say you are unworthy and the other may say you are worthy because you live up to earthly criteria. When I first found the teachings of the ascended masters, I knew the masters teach at a high level and the organization I had found had a pretty elaborate set of requirements. My unworthy self tried to convince me that I would never be able to live up to the requirements and that I might as well not get involved with another spiritual organization. It would only end in disappointment, as I had experienced with the meditation movement.

In retrospect, I have no doubt that joining this new movement was part of my divine plan, as was leaving it later. Once my outer mind tuned in to this, the unworthy self stepped back for the time being and the worthy self stepped up to the plate. The worthy self sought to convince me that joining the new movement was good and that I would be able to live up to all of its demands. In fact, it wanted me to believe I would do great because I was a good student with a willingness to walk the path. It was seeking to tempt me with me-esteem.

This may seem to contradict what I said about the human self not wanting us to make spiritual progress, but let's take a closer look. The worthy self might have taken over, but the unworthy self did not disappear. It was still working under the surface, and what it did was to give me a subtle fear of making a mistake in this new organization. After all, if I had found the highest possible spiritual teachers but failed to live up to their requirements, what could be more devastating than that?

I eventually began to see how the two divisions of the human self might seem to be opposites but they work towards the same goal. I was now in a situation where I had a sense of me-esteem, but it was bought at a price. I had to constantly live up to a set of outer requirements because the cost of failing to do so was very high. This kept me in a tense state where I was always seeking to do what the worthy self wanted me to do in order to avoid the condemnation of the unworthy self. It was a classic good-cop, bad-cop act.

Following the outer requirements did give me genuine spiritual progress and it did raise my consciousness. However, there also came a point where I simply could not make more progress by continuing with this approach. When my human self could not stop me from taking another step forward on my personal path, it attempted to make this the last step. It used the carrot that I was capable of living up to the outer rules and the stick of a potential failure to make me believe that I had now found the highest teaching and thus I needed to continue doing what I was doing for the rest of my life.

This would never have gotten me beyond a certain level of consciousness, meaning my human self would have stopped my progress and kept itself alive. In order to accomplish this goal, my human self had to morph into a more spiritual version based on the teachings I had found, but that wasn't very difficult. Once it felt I was no longer growing, it felt quite secure in this new position. Instead of shifting my sense of self towards the pure self, I had simply created a more sophisticated human self that was good at appearing to be very spiritual.

This was a gilded cage. I could feel very spiritual, but in reality I was trapped. The fear of failing to live up to outer requirements was so severe—because I would seemingly lose everything I had gained—that for a time it prevented me from questioning my approach to spirituality. This prevented me from shifting from my human self towards my pure self. The stalemate lasted several years and I have seen the same thing happen to others. In fact, I think all of us will have to go through this phase, and we might call it one of the important initiations on the path. Will we allow ourselves to get stuck at a certain level instead of asking the questions that can help us move on?

In my experience, there is only one way out of this stalemate, and it is to bond with your Christ self. Since that happened to me, I feel as if my Christ self has given me a constant frame of reference. It is not that my Christ self gives me verbal instructions that I can grasp and analyze with the human mind. It is more like a subtle inner sense that now it is time to take the next step on my path. When I tune in to my Christ self, I clearly sense when it is time to move on from a given situation, and so far this has helped me go through some major changes in my life, such as ending a marriage and moving from the United States back to Europe. I have also gone through some equally great shifts in my sense of self, including accepting my potential to serve the ascended masters in a more direct capacity.

Your own private universe

After you start tuning in to your Christ self and the ascended masters, you will be guided through a process of reevaluating your entire approach to spirituality. In my case, one of the aspects I had to look at was whether I would continue to use my involvement with a spiritual movement in a never-ending quest to defend my fragile sense of me-esteem and we-esteem. The alternative was to step up to a new approach where I was focused on shifting out of the human self that needs me-esteem and we-esteem so I could discover my spiritual self and thereby gain true self-esteem.

What helped me was a specific teaching of the Buddha. The most well-known Buddhic scripture is the Dhammapadha. There are many different translations of it, but I found a version in which the opening verse talks about mental states that spring from perception but cannot override perception. This hit me and I kept pondering it for a period of time. I eventually saw that I am the center of my own private universe.

You may recall that during the Middle Ages people believed the earth was the center of the universe with the sun and all the stars revolving around it. We were so important, they thought, that God had made our planet the center of everything. Well, I began to see that my human self has created its own version of this view because I am the center of my own private universe. You, of course, are the center of your private universe as is everyone else on this planet. My private universe is not a real universe—it is a *perceived* universe. It is a universe that exists only in my mind.

It is a universe that is created by my own perception, by the way I see the world. As the Buddha said: First there is my perception and my perception gives rise to my mental state. Once I am in that mental state, I cannot question the perception that created it and thus I cannot get out of that mental state. I am trapped, and this causes all of my suffering.

As a personal example, I had created my own world view based on my upbringing in Denmark. As with most of us, I had been programmed with certain views of life, and I took them for granted. I could not even think of questioning them. I simply did not see there was another way to look at life than the way I had been exposed to since childhood.

After I moved to the United States I was exposed to so many new circumstances, which I never would have experienced in Denmark, that I very clearly realized that people in a larger country have a vastly different world view. The advantage for me was that I had no personal history. No one knew me and I had no expectations to fulfill. It was literally like starting life anew on a clean white page. I could re-create myself any way I wanted regardless of how I had come to see myself and how other people had come to see me during my upbringing.

I did indeed re-create myself. Because I moved to the United States only to follow my spiritual quest, I re-created myself as an entirely spiritual person. After I moved back to Europe and visited Denmark, I realized that I had not yet resolved all aspects of the personality I had created as I was growing up. At least I could see this old personality, though, whereas when I lived in Denmark I simply could not see how it was limiting me in many ways. It was so familiar or normal to me that I could not even conceive that I could be a different kind of person than the one I was brought up to be. In the language I am using in this book, I would explain this in terms of the four levels of the mind and how they form a hierarchical structure.

My basic perception of life is determined by my sense of identity, which is the way I look at myself, God and life. This sets a pattern for everything that happens at the mental, emotional and conscious levels. My basic perception of life creates my mental/emotional state. Once that state has been created, my conscious mind is so focused on dealing with the demands of the mental/emotional state that it simply has no attention left over for questioning the perception (sense of identity) that created its situation. As a result, I am trapped in dealing with the results of my perception, but I can never really change my life because I cannot go high enough to change the perception.

As an example, let's consider the fact that most of us were brought up to see ourselves as human beings who are severely limited by the capabilities of our physical bodies and by certain norms in our families and society. In reality, we are spiritual beings who are not bound by anything in the material world, and this is precisely what the Buddha, Jesus and other spiritual teachers have attempted to show us. We have simply come to identify ourselves as human beings, and this traps us in the duality of the human self. This basic perception of life—that we are human beings, limited by material circumstances—now creates a mental/emotional state.

In this state, we have an unworthy human self that says we are no good and we have a worthy human self that is seeking to build esteem through some standard in this world. There is a constant tension and battle between the two, and we are trapped in the pattern of seeking to run away from or silence the unworthy self by living up to the never-ending demands of the worthy self. We are trapped in the mental state of non-peace that comes from the divided (dualistic) perception of the human self.

This frantic quest for building an ever-threatened and fragile sense of me-esteem and we-esteem eats up our attention, and we never have any energy left over for standing back and asking ourselves: "Why am I doing this?" We never actually question the boundaries we have been brought up to accept as being absolute. I love the old quote by Henry Ford: "Whether you believe you *can* or whether you believe you *can't*, you're right!"

Seeing your perception filter

I am standing in the center of my private universe. As I look at life, it is as if I see a universe that is centered around "me." I put "me" in quotation marks because it is really the human self. My human self forms a filter around my pure self. It is like standing in the center of a circular building and I can only see the surrounding world through the windows in the building. First of all, not all wall spaces have windows, so there are some aspects of life that are simply blocked from my view. But the windows that are there are not clear. They are covered with a film that either colors or distorts what I see through them.

As an example, let me describe my family in Denmark. They have all been born in the same midsized town as their parents and they all still live there. Most of them will likely die there as well. My family members come from a working-class background and as I was growing up, it was unthinkable to start your own business. It was also unthinkable to look for a better job in a nearby town or to move to another part of the country. You were born in that town and that's where you were expected to live and work your entire life.

As a visual illustration, imagine one of my family members standing inside his own personal house. The house is circular and it has windows all around, so theoretically you can see all of life's possibilities. During his upbringing, this person has had most of the windows painted over so he can see only a small fraction of the total possibilities available to him. Thus, he defines himself as an inhabitant of this little town and he can see no other possibility than taking whatever jobs are available there for the rest of his life. Mind you, I am not saying there is necessarily anything wrong with this. I have great respect for the law of free will. All I am saying is that we are all limited by our upbringings, but for those of us who are spiritual, I think we have opened our minds to the possibility that we can clean some of the windows in our private house and expand our view of life.

We are all standing in the center of our human self, and all we can see of the world is what our human self lets through. What our human self does let through is colored in ways that we do not see. Based on this limited and flawed perception, we are supposed to react to what happens in life and we are supposed to somehow find a way to be happy and feel that our life has meaning. How on earth did we all get fooled into calling this "normal," even calling it life? There must be a better way!

When I was a child my father would tell me stories about his childhood, including how he was mistreated by the teachers in school. The result was that he refused to learn and left school after the seventh grade. He also told me how he had read books about people traveling the world, and he told me how his dream was to have become an engineer building bridges all over the world. Well, even at an early age I could see that if you leave school early because you rebel against the teachers, you have no chance of becoming an engineer. I knew it was my father's psychological reaction to his school that caused him to abort his own life's dream. We human beings are limited by our psychological conditions and it is these conditions that cause us to make ourselves and each other miserable. My spiritual path has only made me even more aware of how everything in our lives revolves around our psycho-spiritual topography.

When I think about this, there are times where I almost feel a sense of hopelessness, a sense of: "How will this ever get better?" I am wounded because my parents did certain things to me. They did not do this out of evil intent but because they were wounded. My parents were wounded because their parents were wounded. Thus what we pass on from generation to generation is the same wounds and the same divisions of the human self. How will we ever get out of this mess?

When I feel this way, I only need to tune in to my Christ self, which is what Jesus called the "comforter." And truly, it is comforting to directly experience that I have a way to heal my wounds and transcend my past. Since my therapy, I have been aware of just how many psychological wounds I have healed in this lifetime, and I believe we are all capable of this.

When I look at how many spiritual people are working so hard to rise above their limitations, I do feel a real hope that the world not only can change but is, in fact, already changing. This makes life livable and gives hope for a better future.

Taking responsibility for perception

Seeing the influence of my perception filter with the help of my Christ self has also helped me recognize that everything that happens on this planet has no ultimate reality. The earth is almost like a sandbox, where we may seem to have great power, but in reality none of what we do here can influence our spiritual selves or our pure selves. Our human selves can be hurt by other human selves, but our human selves are not real and have no permanence. No matter what wound we have in our human selves, we can never lose the ability to simply step outside that perception filter and reconnect to pure awareness. Every wound in the human self is not a real hurt; it is only a perceived hurt. I know this can sound harsh, but it is only harsh as long as you identify with the human self.

After guiding me to the Buddhic teachings on perception, my Christ self helped me come to an inner realization. I have often had breakthroughs after invoking light in my spiritual practice because it clears away negative energies and stills the mind, making it far easier to hear my inner teacher. One day after I had been using the spoken word through decrees, I felt very calm and I suddenly felt my Christ self sending me a thought impulse that became translated into words as follows:

No one ever did anything to you!

My first reaction was the human self going into absolute panic and starting to argue against this: "What do you mean, no one ever did anything to me? Of course people have done all kinds of things to me. Just look at all the evil going on on this planet. Are you saying the Nazis didn't do anything to the Jews when they shoved them into the gas chambers. This is just the worst nonsense I have ever heard." At this point I was able to detach myself from this reaction and just watch my human self ramble on. I felt completely still, and I just sat there until the ripples on the water of my emotions died down. Then I took a neutral look at this statement and I started to see what it actually means.

Our perception is like standing inside a house where the windows only let through a limited view of the surroundings, and what they do let through is colored and distorted. Now imagine that someone does something to your physical body. Our normal reaction would be to say that the person "did

something to me." As spiritual people we gradually stop identifying ourselves with the physical body. We become aware that
we are each a spiritual being who is residing in a body.

When someone does something to my body, the self that
I am does not directly experience what happens to the body. I
experience this only through the perception filter of my human
self. In other words, the "house" that makes up my perception
filter is my human self, and my physical body is actually outside
that filter. Even if you hurt my physical body, what I experience is not your action but a reaction to your action.

This reaction takes place in and is shaped by my human
self, my perception filter. My action creates an energy impulse,
so to speak, that is sent into my mind. As the energy impulse
passes through my perception filter, it is changed and potentially distorted by my human self. What I experience is not
what you did but how my human self *reacted* to what you did.

Let me illustrate this by comparing it to physical sight.
When I was a child, I was told that my eyes see. If I am looking at a sunset, it is my eyes that are seeing the sunset. I started
realizing the fallacy of this when I got into photography. I can
use a camera to take a picture of a sunset or a garbage can in a
back alley, but the camera can't tell the difference. It is a purely
mechanical device, and so are my eyes.

My eyes are mechanical devices that register light rays that
enter them from the outside. My retina converts those physical
light rays to a signal that is not unlike the digital signals used
by computers. These signals are then passed on through the
brain's circuitry to the visual cortex. This part of my brain is in
complete darkness, shielded by my skull. My visual cortex does
not see the light rays that enter my eyes. It receives data signals
and then it converts them to an image that is displayed inside

my brain. If I am looking at a sunset, my eyes are *not* seeing the sunset. They register light rays, convert them into signals and pass them on to the brain. My brain then takes this data, uses it to display a picture inside itself and then it calls this image "a sunset."

What if the data sent by my eyes somehow got distorted so that the image displayed by my brain is not exactly the same as what is coming into my eyes? Philosophers have philosophized about this topic for centuries. How can we ever know that when you and I look at the color green, we see the exact same color? We may agree that grass is green, but what if your brain makes green seem darker than what I see?

As a real-life example, consider digital cameras. Such cameras don't simply take a picture of what a forest or flower looks like. The image taken by the camera is affected by a computer program, an algorithm. Some cameras are programmed to make green colors more green and others to make red colors appear more red. Also consider how your computer can adjust a picture and make it lighter or darker and change the color balance.

Your perception filter is what your subconscious mind does to everything that happens to you, much like the program that manipulates the pictures from your digital camera. When you learn to be aware of your perception filter, you can consciously change your perception of a situation, just as you use a computer to adjust a photo. Now take this one step further. If your brain displays an image of a sunset, some part of your mind may attach a value-laden label to it and call it "beautiful." If your brain displays an image of a back alley, your mind may label this "ugly." This is not done by your visual cortex. In fact, scientists who study the brain can't really say which part of the brain actually does this. I believe this labeling does not happen in the brain but in the human self.

The central function of the human self is that it not only labels things, but that it also attaches a value-driven judgment to them. Imagine yourself looking at a table. Your mind is probably neutral when it comes to tables, but your mind is not neutral when it comes to sunsets and back alleys strewn with garbage. In such cases, the human self simply has to apply a value-driven overlay. And this is the point about a perception filter.

Your pure self is standing in the center of the house made up by the human self. You can only see those aspects of life that your human self lets through. What it does let through might be distorted in ways you cannot easily determine. And on top of that, what the human self perceives is colored by an overlay that puts everything on a scale with two extremes: good and evil, right and wrong, beautiful and ugly, dangerous and safe—and a million other such judgments.

Based on this highly distorted image, you are supposed to make good decisions about how to respond to life. At one point I literally saw that no one had ever done anything to me because everything that had happened to me had been filtered through my human self.

Yes, certain children might have teased me in school, but it was my human self who had created the image of what had happened and had then applied a value judgment to it. I had actually learned at an early age that if I did not allow myself to feel teased, I could avoid giving the bullies their satisfaction and then they would leave me alone. I literally saw that other people had never done anything to me because I had done something to myself.

What had affected me was not what other people did but how I had *perceived* what they did. That perception took place exclusively in my own mind— and that is why it was my human self that had an impact on my psychology, my perception of life and my sense of self. I have done everything to myself.

You might remember that I earlier said that if you want to become aware of how your human self reacts, you could monitor your reactions to what you would read. Well, take a few seconds to feel how your mind responds to what I just said. Is there a part of your mind that wants to deny this? Is there a part that simply rejects this on emotional grounds and a part that mounts all kinds of intellectual arguments against it? If so, you have now become aware of two aspects of your human self. They are desperate to remain unnoticed by you and that is why they want you to deny what you just read.

When I came to the realization that no one had ever done anything to me, I saw that this was the most liberating thing that had ever happened to me. Why? Because it showed me that my experience of life—my *life* experience—is not caused by anything that happens to me in the material world. My experience of life is caused exclusively by my own mind. This is liberating because I cannot control what other people do to me or what physical events I might experience. But I do have the potential to take command over my own state of mind.

If I become aware that my human self distorts my perception and makes me feel bad about certain situations, I can use spiritual and psychological tools (decrees, study, therapy, etc.) to dissolve that aspect of my human self. I can then go through the same situation without being affected by it in a negative way, without having a hurtful emotional reaction. I can become like the Buddha who could face the demons of

Mara without reacting in a way that gave them power over him. This gives me the potential to experience myself as a pure self instead of experiencing myself through the perception filter of the human self.

Experiencing myself as a pure self is the only way to transcend the me-esteem and we-esteem that can only be defined in relation to something in this world. My human self will never attain true self-esteem, because it must come from beyond this world. It must come from my spiritual self, which I can experience only when I pull my pure self outside the perception filter of the human self. The beauty of this is that I don't have to dissolve all aspects of my human self in order to have this experience. I only have to dissolve enough so that my pure self is not pulled entirely into the human self. I just need to lessen the magnetic pull so that I can occasionally step outside the chaos of the human self and experience a more pure form of self.

The human self can control me only as long as it is hidden to my pure self. Becoming aware that I have a human self and that it colors my perception is an important step. I can then start questioning my perception. As I invoke spiritual light to reduce the magnetic pull of lower energies and as I use spiritual teachings and my inner guidance to question my illusions, I can begin to clean the windows through which I perceive the world. When I then become aware of how my perception filter colors my reaction to certain situations, I can consciously step outside my perception filter and see its unreality. As I do this, I am building a positive momentum that will eventually lead me to discard all illusions in my perception filter.

Keys from Chapter 5

◊ **When we rise above some of the lower energies** and illusions we hold on to, we see that the real goal of spiritual growth is to overcome all attachments to things in the material world.

◊ **The human self uses many subtle illusions** in an attempt to control us. It hides behind illusions so that we never see the human self and how it influences us. The human self will even use a spiritual teaching to camouflage itself.

◊ **The key to overcoming attachments** is to see that they are a product of your perception, how you see yourself and life.

◊ **We each have a private universe** created by our human self. It forms a filter that colors how we look at everything.

◊ **No one ever did anything to us.** What affects us is how we react to external events, and our reaction is a product of our perception filter.

6 | The DIRECT EXPERIENCE of YOUR TRUE SELF

When you begin to grasp the importance of questioning your perception, you will rise to a new level on the spiritual path and you will feel like a lot of new opportunities open up to you. Before you start questioning your perception, you think that the way you see things is the way things are. You can't change the way things are, so you can't change the way you react to most situations—you feel stuck.

After you see the need to question your perception filter, you realize you are never stuck. No matter what the outer situation might be, you always have the option of looking at the way you react to the situation. Your reaction is determined by your perception filter and by questioning the way you look at things, you will see what you could not see before. As Wayne Dyer likes to say: "When you change the way you look at things, the things you look at change."

After I started seeing the need to question my perception, it became clear that there is another veil of illusion we must walk through before we can find true self-esteem. I have said that we can become trapped into seeing the spiritual path as a quest to do more and more. We can also be trapped into thinking it is a matter of finding the ultimate guru or belief system. Beyond that is the much more subtle illusion of thinking the goal of the spiritual path is to perfect the separate self so that it can gain entry into the spiritual realm.

I've already explained why the separate self cannot enter the spiritual realm and must be left behind. What is the central problem in seeking to perfect the separate self? It is that the separate self is essentially nothing more than its perception filter. When you look at life through the filter, you will see everything a certain way and you will think what you see is ultimate reality.

If you are wearing yellow glasses, you will think that the problem is that things are not yellow enough so you need to "perfect" the glasses by making them even more yellow. The real problem is not that the glasses aren't good enough, but that they aren't real. Thus, the true road to self-esteem is not to perfect the human self but to take off the glasses of the human perception filter.

This may seem self-evident to some, but it didn't seem so to me. It took me over 20 years of walking the spiritual path to come to the point where I started seeing the importance of perception filters. When I finally did see this, I felt like I had gone through a major transformation. It was as if I could see for the first time how to make progress. Instead of hoping for some miracle to raise my consciousness, I now knew I had the power in my own mind to become aware of my perception filter and systematically dismantle my colored perceptions by questioning my unrecognized beliefs.

I also realized, somewhat painfully, that many of my efforts on the path only had the effect of "spiritualizing" my human self, causing it to take on the appearance of being spiritual. I literally saw how I had attempted to create a spiritual self or persona that could live up to all of the criteria defined by the spiritual teachings I had been studying. This was, in fact, a liberating realization because I became aware of how much tension I had felt as I was going through this process. I understood that the cause of the tension was that I intuitively knew I was on the wrong track, but my outer mind had not been able to see why. Thus, I had been thinking that the only way to make progress was to do more of what I had been doing.

I now saw that the real way to make progress was to do something that was at a higher level, namely questioning my most subtle beliefs, the perceptions I had been taking for granted. This turned out to be very freeing because instead of trying to force myself into this mold of how a "good spiritual student" should be, I could begin to consider who I really am and how I want to be. At one point I understood that seeking to follow all of the rules given by a spiritual organization was like seeking to force my body into one of these medieval suits of armor; people were smaller in the old days and I simply wouldn't be able to fit into that mold.

At a certain stage of my path, following the outer rules had been useful to me. But I had now reached a stage where I could not progress by following rules. I had to go within, make contact with my real self and then dare to express that instead of blindly following rules. Of course, what stood between me and my real self was precisely the perception filter of my human self.

Become aware of the ego

The first time I became aware of perception filters was when my history teacher told us that during the Middle Ages people believed the earth was flat. In today's world, we have other perception filters that are equally primitive—only we tend to think they are not perception filters but accurate descriptions of reality (just as people in the Dark Ages thought their perceptions were reality). For example, it is amazing to me that there is a new brand of atheists who seem very intent on tearing down religion, even labeling religion as the cause of all human conflict.

These new atheists insist that science has proven that there is nothing beyond the material universe and that any idea of a spiritual world is just a subjective belief. At the same time, these people insist we live in a world that was not created by design but is the result of essentially random processes. If everything is random, then what sense does it make to say that their idea of atheism is an objective truth and that any idea of a spiritual world is subjective perception? If we live in a random world, then there can be no absolute or final truth and everything is a matter of perception.

The new atheists also claim that any spiritual beliefs are the result of flaws in our DNA. Yet if DNA is created through a random process, then how can we say that the DNA of a spiritual person is flawed whereas the DNA of an atheist is the way it should be? If these new atheists are right, then they have negated their own argument because the consequence of their claims is that any human belief is the result of a random process in a universe where there is no design and thus no ultimate reality. In other words, the new atheists are essentially saying:

"Your spiritual beliefs are subjective, but my atheist beliefs are objective." But beyond that, they are saying: "My random DNA is better than your random DNA and thus my atheist beliefs are right but your spiritual beliefs are wrong."

My vision is that we are all trapped inside our personal universes and we each have a personal perception filter that colors the way we see everything. This perception filter is not coded into our DNA and it is not the result of random or designed processes beyond our control. Instead, the perception filter is coded into our human selves, but it became so as a result of choices we made in the past. That means we can free ourselves from our perception filters by making choices in the present.

The essential promise of the spiritual path is that we have the potential to go through a gradual process of freeing ourselves from our perception filters until we see the world without the filters created by the human self. To me, this is what the Buddha, Jesus and many other spiritual teachers came to demonstrate. They showed us a way to look at the world that is above and beyond the dualistic, self-centered view of the human self. They showed us that we are all more than human beings, that we all have a potential to rise above the human state of consciousness.

I am not saying that I right now have no perception filter. I can say that over the past 36 years, I have had the direct experience that it is possible for me to raise my perception so I can go beyond some of my self-centered ways of looking at the world. I have also experienced that by systematically purifying my perception, I have become able to grasp many ideas I never understood in the past. I have also been able to overcome many of my psychological wounds and free myself from the kind of behavior patterns that caused my own inner suffering and caused me to have conflicts with other people. I also know hundreds of people who have applied the same process, and this gives me a real sense that we human beings do have the potential to rise above conflict and create a more peaceful society. Truly, the cause of conflict is not religion but a mechanism in the human psyche, namely the ego. By becoming aware of the ego and systematically leaving behind elements of the human self, we can indeed free ourselves from this perpetual human power struggle that the Buddha called the "Sea of Samsara." For that to happen, we really do need to come to see the beam (ego) in our own eyes.

Listening for your inner guidance

It is all well and good to see the human self in other people, but we will not actually make progress on our personal path until we can see an element of our own human self and leave it behind. Nothing has helped me see my own ego more than the direct inner guidance of my Christ self and the ascended masters. It is not that the masters or my Christ self come across as a booming voice from heaven that mercilessly exposes my ego. Instead, my Christ self gives me an inner frame of reference that there is something beyond my subjective perception. This can often be subtle, and it took me some time to recognize how inner guidance works.

We all have inner guidance, although some people don't recognize it. The major issue is that we often expect that our inner guidance will conform to our human perception filter. The entire purpose of inner guidance is to set us free from our human perception, and how could it do that by conforming to and thus validating our perception filter? Inner guidance must offer us an alternative to our perception filter, and if we are not open to this, we simply will not notice the guidance.

I came to a point where I recognized that all of my life two distinct phenomena had been occurring in my mind. One was that I would often experience a very gentle inner voice giving me thoughts that took the form of words. One example of this was when for several months I was contemplating the concept of God's will. At the time, I was studying a spiritual teaching that presented God's will as an external will and our only choice was total submission or total rebellion. This created a conflict in me because I have always sensed that I am responsible for making my own decisions. So I could not see how it could be right to surrender my individual will to this external being and essentially put on a straitjacket.

After being perplexed by this for a time, I one day got to a point where I said: "Okay, God, just show me what your will is for my life and I'll do it." After this moment of surrender, I "heard" a gentle inner voice form the words: "What if it is God's will that you make your own decisions?" At first this shocked me, but after pondering it I saw it was a higher view. It is indeed God's will that I make my own decisions because that is the only way I can learn and therefore raise my consciousness. The highest will of God is that we all raise our consciousness by exercising the free will God has given us.

Since that incident, I've recognized that I've had this inner voice my entire life. In many situations, I either would not pay attention or I would use the outer, rational mind to argue against what I received from my inner voice. Some of my biggest mistakes came after I argued against my inner voice. For example, I was once faced with a situation where I had to either leave the United States or find a way to obtain a green card. A person presented me with a way that he said was officially illegal but unofficially tolerated. My inner voice clearly told me this was not a good step but I used my outer mind to argue it into oblivion. This did indeed cause me severe problems later and it took me many years to fully leave behind the consequences.

I have also realized you cannot necessarily follow the inner voice literally. For instance, I was once given the opportunity to work for a company for a short time. My outer mind argued that this was not a good job, but I felt an intuitive prompting to take the job. On the first day I met a person who offered me a much better job. Had I not decided to accept the first job, I would not have met that person. Despite what my outer mind thought, it was literally a good job. You have to find a certain balance—being willing to make decisions based on what you know even though you do not know everything. Your inner voice is not a fortune teller that gives you detailed directions. It sometimes simply tells you to "Start walking," and only when you are moving will you receive directions for where to go next.

How we receive guidance

There are two phenomena that give us inner guidance. Hearing an inner voice is relatively concrete, but the other factor is much more subtle. Another way we receive inner guidance is actually experiencing a state of consciousness that is beyond the normal, namely what I have called pure awareness or the pure state of the self. It can be as a sense of witnessing a situation from the outside, a sense of being connected to something greater than yourself, a sense of inner peace or a sense of heightened perception or awareness. At one point in my life I was faced with a group of people who were leveling some pretty aggressive accusations against me on the internet. I was feeling like I had a dilemma because as long as I did not respond, they could make up all kinds of things (which they did) and get away with it. On the other hand, I knew I did not want to enter into a dualistic fight of trying to prove them wrong for their attempts to prove me wrong. One day I was lying on my bed and spontaneously said: "I AM Presence, how do you look at this situation?"

Take note of how open-ended that question was. I was not saying: "Show me what to do in this situation." I was simply asking for a different perspective. I then instantly felt like I was lifted high above the earth and I was looking down on the situation from a great distance. I saw how insignificant the situation was, seen from a larger perspective. I also saw how, even though it seemed serious at the time, it would have very little impact on the totality of this lifetime or my greater spiritual growth. While this did not actually change the outer situation, it did give me a sense of peace that the storm would blow over and sunny skies would return.

Another time I felt this more subtle form of guidance was when I was being accused by the leader of a spiritual group for doing something I had not actually done. As she was yelling at me, I did not go into the normal sense of wanting to get away or defend myself. Instead, I felt complete inner calm. It was as if I was a detached observer of the situation. I saw that she was simply taking her personal frustrations out on me. I also saw that her work was important and that she needed my continued support. Instead of defending myself or becoming angry, I reacted with gentleness and it calmed her down. We were then able to move on and actually do the work we had set out to do.

Our personal path can be seen as a string of choices. It is as if we are walking down a path and suddenly it divides into two—we have to choose one fork in the road or the other. In such situations, there is usually one choice that the human self wants us to make and it argues for this with a very loud voice, seeking to manipulate us by appealing to fear, pride, anger, pity or whatever mechanism has worked before. If we pay attention, there will also be something—either a gentle inner voice or a subtle sensation—that offers us an alternative to the boisterous voice of the human self.

Our first task is to learn to recognize this alternative voice and then start to follow it. Beyond that, we can learn to expose the human self by paying attention to the contrast between the voice of the human self and the inner voice. I have learned that I am never in a situation where I do not have both options: outer and inner guidance. It is simply up to me to decide to pay attention to the inner voice and to follow it instead of the outer voice of the human self.

The illusion of perfecting the human self

The human self is essentially a conglomerate of beliefs and perceptions that color the way you look at everything. If you broke down every one of these perceptions and beliefs, there would be no substance at all to the human self. After I started identifying my human self as a distinct voice that was in contrast to my inner voice, I also began seeing a very subtle mechanism. I had seen that it was impossible to perfect the human self, but the next step was to see why this is so. The deeper reason is that the human self is based on the underlying perception that it is *a separate self.*

What the human self is doing is that it is trying to qualify for entry into "heaven" based on its underlying perception that it is a separate self. This is what Albert Einstein expressed when he said that we can't solve a problem with the same state of consciousness that created the problem. "Being saved," "entering heaven" or "attaining enlightenment" are simply coded messages that really mean "entering into oneness." How can you enter into oneness based on the perception that you are a separate self?

The human self was created based on the perception that it is separate. The human self can never overcome this perception because doing so would mean that the human self would cease to exist. The human self has a survival instinct, so it will resist this realization for dear life. How does it resist? Well, in many ways. One is to create the entire impression of a false path to salvation, namely that if only you can make your human self live up to a standard defined by the ultimate religion or guru, it will qualify for entry into heaven. In other words, it tries to convince you of the belief that you can enter heaven without consciously dealing with and dismissing the illusion of separation.

The human self is seeking to attain a state of perfection, but this state is defined by the perception filter of the separate self. Your definition of perfection will seem completely real to you, but it has no connection to the reality of what it takes to pass the final exam in Terra University. You are essentially using a flawed perception to try to create the impression of perfection. You are seeking to force the universe to fit into your mental box and it will never fit. The earth was still round when everyone believed it to be flat. How do we escape this trap? A good start is to use our ability to reason so we can actually come to see the inconsistencies and flaws in our perception filters.

It is perfectly possible for us to see how one aspect of the human self is in constant opposition to another aspect. For example, during my therapy I saw how I had created two aspects of my human self to deal with the two dominant role models I had as a child, namely my father and my uncle. They had been in constant competition with each other for their entire lives, and I had one aspect of my human self that reacted as my father and another that reacted as my uncle.

My therapist helped me see that the conflict could never be resolved because both aspects of the human self were created from an illusion. There really was no conflict and there was no ultimate solution. I simply needed to see the futility of it and walk away from both aspects of my human self.

Seeing something with our reasoning faculties does not necessarily mean we can let go of it. For me, reasoning has always been a first step and a very necessary step, but the ultimate release comes when I directly experience a reality that is beyond the human self. Once we are enveloped in our perception filter, how do we connect to a reality that is beyond the filter? The key is to have what has traditionally been called a mystical experience and which I have called a breakthrough experience.

Having mystical experiences

I discovered the spiritual path at the age of 18 when I read the book *Autobiography of a Yogi* by the Indian mystic

Paramahansa Yogananda. In the book, he describes a number of mystical experiences and this resonated strongly with me because I had such experiences during my childhood. Shortly after reading the book and becoming involved with the meditation movement (which had no connection to Yogananda), I had several mystical experiences, even one where I left my body and entered a golden light.

Even though these experiences happened spontaneously, they were rare, and I quickly found that when I tried to have more experiences it was impossible to force them. The harder I tried, the more they moved away. My human self combined this experience with the traditional image of a remote God and I developed the attitude that God was seeking to hide itself from me.

As a result, I did what I have seen many other seekers do: I developed an approach to spirituality that basically ignored God. In the mediation movement this was easy because we never used the word God but talked about "Creative Intelligence." This approach was appropriate for me at the time because I was not ready to deal with my relationship to God. As a young child, I had a very innocent relationship with God because I felt there was a divine presence that was always with me. This wasn't like a magic helper that did things for me; it was simply a comforting presence.

As I started learning about religion in school, I quickly felt there was something completely wrong with the way Christianity portrays God. My childhood experience of a comforting presence simply could not be reconciled with the Judeo-Christian image of an all-male angry and judgmental God residing in a distant heaven, leaving us alone to wallow in our own misery. As a child how could I deal with the fact that the remote God was being forced upon me with such authority? How could I say that thousands of years of religious tradition were just plain out of touch with the reality of how God is? I couldn't, so I started ignoring the question of God.

When I found the teachings of the ascended masters, this attitude started to shift because these teachings did talk about God. For several years I was so focused on the masters that I could still largely ignore my feelings about God. But after I bonded with my Christ self, it became clear to me that I would never go beyond a certain point on the spiritual path unless I resolved all conflicts in my view of God.

I would even say that you cannot develop true self-esteem unless you make peace with God. The reason is that ultimate self-esteem can come only from full knowledge of the self. The deeper reality is that the pure self is an extension of your spiritual self, which is an extension of God. The unifying element behind all form and behind all self-aware beings is God. As the ancient Vedas say, there is only one self.

A mystical experience is, in essence, an experience where the pure self steps outside its perception filter and directly experiences a higher reality. Our perception filters are created from the illusion that we are separate beings. The deeper reality is that all life is one and is one with God. I started seeing that as long as I maintain an approach to spirituality that ignores God, I am trying to do the impossible. If I say I want mystical experiences but am not willing to work on my relationship with God, I am being inconsistent.

A mystical experience takes me closer to oneness, which is God. If I have not made peace with God, I will subconsciously resist coming closer to this entity up there in the sky, which means my lack of resolution will block my mystical experiences. I become trapped in another artificial conflict between two aspects of my human self, one which resists the angry sky-god and one which wants God to step in and magically solve all of its problems. Both of these deny mystical oneness.

The real God does not live up to any of these images, but until I resolve my false images and open my mind to a direct experience of what God is really like, I cannot have this experience. I came to see that God will never force itself upon us. It is up to us to make ourselves ready so the real God can appear. To make ourselves ready truly means removing the artificial elements of the human self that block the inner experience of oneness. Once the blockages are removed, the sunlight of our higher selves will naturally shine through to our conscious minds.

The process of surrendering the ego

An important step for me was to understand the importance of surrender, and again my Christ self guided me to certain teachings given by the ascended masters. What I have described up until now is a series of steps that led me to take full responsibility for my psychology and my path—and it is essential to take this responsibility. Taking full responsibility for our psychology and our own growth is essential, but it is only an intermediate step. The next logical phase on our path is that after we have taken full responsibility, we then give it away again by surrendering ourselves completely unto God. Does this sound paradoxical? Well, it is meant to, but the following will show you how to resolve the paradox.

Consider this idea: You cannot give away what you do not own. I've said that our current situation is a product of choices we have made in the past. We chose to accept certain beliefs based on the illusion of separation and we have mis-qualified energy through those beliefs. For example, you may have accepted the belief that as a warrior you have the right to kill other people for a just cause, but you still misqualify energy by killing people. We cannot surrender until we have taken responsibility and acknowledged that we entered our current mindset by making certain choices. The next step is to transcend those choices, and we do that by surrendering the human self, the ego.

It is this process of surrendering elements of the human self that the rest of this chapter is about. I will describe the steps that led me to see the need to surrender the human self and also experience a major breakthrough of total surrender. However, while I did come to a point of completely surrender-ing myself to God, it would be naive to think that this ends the process of surrender. As long as we are in embodiment here on earth, surrender is an ongoing process. We must constantly surrender and be on guard against forming new attachments.

Once we have understood that surrender, although it might sound like a passive measure, is the ultimate power on the spiritual path, we find it much easier to let go. The more we surrender, the easier it becomes to surrender more. It is like walking up a steep trail and suddenly realizing your pockets are full of sand. You throw out some of the sand and you feel lighter. How long does it take before you realize that the more sand you "surrender," the easier it will be to climb the path?

One might say that here is the key that could make the rest of this chapter unnecessary—the realization that what is holding us back on the spiritual path is the baggage we carry around. This weight is the accumulated misqualified energy in the four levels of our minds, our psychological wounds and the beliefs we created in order to deal with those wounds—beliefs about ourselves, God and the world. This baggage is what makes up our perception filter.

Because of free will, no one—not even God—can take our perception filter away from us. The reality is that at some point in the past, we have all made a decision that was not the best possible, a decision that limits us to this day. We will not be free of that decision and its limiting effects until we replace it with a better decision. An essential part of that process is to let go of the old decision, to simply leave it behind.

I have seen many different approaches to the spiritual path. Some people believe they can power their way through and that by doing spiritual techniques or taking courses, they will automatically make progress. It has been my clear observation that you will not be free until the moment you surrender the beliefs that support the illusion that you are separated from your God and from other people.

We cannot "take heaven by force." We can "take" heaven only by letting go of the beliefs that cause us to feel we are not in heaven—the beliefs that make us "take" or cling to something on earth. That is why Jesus said that if you seek to save your life, you shall lose it, but if you are willing to lose your life—that is, your attachments to anything in this world—you shall find eternal life. God will not force us to enter oneness. We must choose to enter. In order to enter "Heaven," meaning the consciousness of oneness, we must be willing to leave the "earth" consciousness, the separate self, behind for good. As Jesus said, we cannot serve two masters—it's not possible to be in two states of consciousness at once. You cannot be in a state of oneness and a state of separation at the same time. Before we can permanently leave the separate consciousness behind, we have to let go of any attachments of the human self. Until we voluntarily surrender all attachments to the earth and to the separate consciousness, we cannot take the final step into the consciousness of oneness.

I have seen many spiritual seekers who have been following a certain teaching or practice for decades, doing everything right according to the outer rules. This can make us think that we are making great progress and are advanced. But even a true and valid spiritual teaching can be used to build more solid walls of attachments around our minds. This explains why Jesus said that unless we become as little children—and stop puffing ourselves up as being so sophisticated that we no longer have to take the basic step of surrendering our all to God—we cannot enter the kingdom.

We cannot save ourselves

We often start out by seeing the spiritual path as an outer path, and sometimes we continue seeing it that way for decades. In reality, the spiritual path is an inner path—a path of overcoming the human self by shedding our perception filter. That means we have everything we need inside ourselves in order to be saved, ascend or enter Nirvana. But we don't have everything inside the *separate* self. As long as we are trapped in the perception filter of the separate self, we simply cannot save ourselves, because the perception filter forms a closed mental box from which we can see no way out.

We do indeed need something from outside the mental box of the separate self, but that something comes to us from inside our own minds. It comes from making an inner contact with our spiritual teachers and Christ selves through mystical or breakthrough experiences. The goal of the spiritual path is to rise above the human, egotistical frame of mind so that we can escape our own human selves. The human self is based on an illusion and it has created innumerable illusions that it seeks to hide behind in order to preserve itself. As long as we are inside the box of such illusions, we simply cannot see the truth of God and we cannot see through the lies of the human self. That is why we need spiritual teachers who have already made the climb and can therefore guide us as we seek to escape the illusions of our perception filters.

By studying the teachings of the ascended masters, I began to understand that the true goal of the spiritual path is the death of the human self so that we can be reborn into a new spiritual awareness in which we see ourselves as part of a larger whole, as part of God. We have a basic problem, however: when we are trapped in our perception filters, our human selves think they know everything. After I started seeing my human self, I saw that it doesn't recognize the need for a spiritual teacher—the human self literally believes it knows everything. I even discovered a part of my human self that thought it was capable of telling God how the universe really should have been designed! Since childhood I had been fascinated by the fact that so many historical events demonstrate the incredible blunders people make when they are blinded by their human selves.

Take, for example, Napoleon and Hitler, who had great power but made incredible mistakes because they were so blinded by their human selves that they lost touch with reality. Looking at my own life, I could see how many times I had made personal mistakes because I allowed my human self to make me believe that I knew better than anyone else or that I could do whatever I wanted and get away with it.

While we are trapped by the human self, we cannot see clearly how to follow the spiritual path. Therefore, we need the guidance of a teacher or teaching that is above the human self and can show us how to escape the subtleties of the ego. In the beginning stages, we simply have to trust the teacher, even if our human selves believe the teacher's guidance is wrong or too extreme. Most people I know did indeed start their path by finding a teacher or book that expanded their awareness beyond the mental box they had before. When we are open to going beyond a certain mental box, we will find the teacher who can take us there.

The spiritual path can be seen as a long string of initiations, situations in which we have to make a choice. Although there are innumerable variations—with each person having his or her own personal tests—the central decision is always this: Will we listen to the voice of the human self, or will we reach beyond it to hear the voice of the spiritual teacher and Christ self? Will we follow the human self or follow the teacher—this is the central question for a spiritual seeker. It is our version of "to be or not to be."

The subtleties of pride

One of the ascended masters coined the saying: "If the teacher be an ant, heed him." The spiritual teacher will often appear in disguise in order to test us for the most dangerous enemy of spiritual growth, namely pride. Many spiritual seekers have no problem taking directions from the person they consider to be their teacher, but they are not willing to listen to advice from someone they consider to be beneath them. I went through the same phase myself until I realized this approach simply would not get me where I wanted to go. Life itself acts as a teacher and that teacher may sometimes take on an unexpected disguise. If I demand that a teacher lives up to certain criteria defined by my human self, I will overlook the teacher who can take me beyond the human self. It is wise to watch out for pride and listen for the teacher disguised as an ant.

Again, this is a balancing act because we cannot accept everything people say to us. Some people simply project their unresolved psychology upon us, seeking to control or change us as a diversion from looking at their own psychology. The teacher may sometimes be disguised as an ant, but not every ant is a teacher.

In order to really make it to a higher spiritual conscious-ness, we have to be willing to surrender every single aspect of the human self. We cannot attain true spiritual awareness by retaining parts of the human self. As long as we seek to justify the human self or think we can perfect the human self, we are not following the true spiritual path. We are following "the way that seemeth right unto a man, but the ends thereof are the ways of death."

The human self cannot lead us to true self-esteem. The brutal fact about spiritual growth is that trying to perfect the human self according to criteria defined by the human self will never get us to a higher state of consciousness. The human self simply has to die. It has to be surrendered, completely and unconditionally. Complete and unconditional surrender of the human self is the core of the spiritual path.

Of course, we can't surrender the human self all at once because that would leave us in a vacuum. When I was in the meditation movement, I heard about a person who had tried to make progress so fast that he lost touch with reality and ended up in a mental institution. This taught me that we all have a need for continuity in our lives. If we got rid of too much of the human self at one time, we would suffer a severe identity crisis. At the same time we surrender parts of our human self, we have to start integrating with a higher part of our being. I have called this the spiritual self or the I AM Presence. The spiritual path is a collaborative effort between our conscious minds and our spiritual teachers—our Christ selves and the ascended masters. After I felt the bonding to my Christ self, I knew I am not walking the path alone.

Everything on earth revolves around our free will. God didn't create our misery—we did by co-creating from the consciousness of separation. In fact, our misery is entirely the creation of our perception filter. We are not actually miserable; we only *perceive* ourselves as such. We have allowed our human selves to trick us into creating a society and culture based on fear and lack. The more we seek to solve our problems without challenging the dualistic belief system of the human self, the more we create new illusions that result in new problems. I began to see how this can create a downward spiral that in the past has caused several civilizations to self-destruct. That applies to our personal lives as well.

Take the example of Hitler and Napoleon, who became so closed to any outside advice that it turned their lives into negative spirals that ended in disaster. My own father had done the same and this trapped him in such a small mental box that he could not even enjoy his retirement, even though it gave him the freedom he had been longing for during his working life.

As I recognized this pattern, I began to feel a very strong urge to escape this merry-go-round of the human self. I came to a "moment of truth" (one among many) in which I felt a determination well up from the bottom of my being. I decided that I was going to take full and complete responsibility for my personal life, my beliefs and illusions, my psychology and my spiritual path. I decided to acknowledge the fact that I had created my current situation, and therefore it is naive to think I could pray to God and he would whisk away all my problems through a miracle.

God gave me free will and he will not violate his own laws. Because I had decided to create the human self and to let it lead me down the garden path of separation, I had created my current situation. Therefore it was up to me to separate myself out from the human self and its illusions so I could begin to create a situation that was not based on fear and lack but on love and oneness.

I also knew that I could not escape the human self on my own. I would need an ascended master and my Christ self— even a living teacher if one was available—to help me escape the labyrinth of ego illusions. The spiritual teachers I chose, however, would not be the common Christian image of a savior who would do all the work for me. I created the human self, and it is up to me to uncreate it. If a master took that self away from me, he or she would be violating God's law of free will. The purpose of free will is to give us the opportunity to learn and I would learn nothing from a master who was taking away my human self. Much of my life had been consumed by futile attempts to defend my human self and maintain its illusions. I saw how I had often been involved with discussions with other people where I was simply seeking to validate my human self or defend it against a perceived attack.

This had consumed so much time and energy that it seemed completely futile. I finally saw these ego-games in all of their mind-numbing insanity and I cried out: *"I can't do this anymore, I don't want to do this anymore—God, help me!"*

Surrendering to God

My process of surrender took some years, but at one point I had an experience of complete and unconditional surrender. All of my life I had been sensing that my life had a purpose, that I had a mission to fulfill. After finding the teachings of the ascended masters, that sense was reinforced as I felt I was one among millions of spiritual people who have volunteered to help take this planet into a higher stage of spiritual development.

Unfortunately, having that strong sense of purpose had actually caused a building sense of frustration because I felt that I had not found my outer service, that I had not done anything significant. After I started pondering the need to surrender everything, I saw that I might also have to surrender my concept of what it meant to do something important. This is an essential point, and I believe it is true for many spiritual seekers. My vision of having something to do was correct, but my human self had created an overlay of how this should be done. This overlay was based on my human perception filter, and the result was that I was pursuing an impossible goal.

I had the "what" part right, but the "how" part was simply out of touch with reality because my human self could not grasp the true contents of my divine plan. This finally came to a head for me, and one day I was sitting in my office meditating on my frustration, and I suddenly saw the futility of thinking my spiritual mission should follow the limited vision of my human self. I saw how my dreams of doing something important were nothing but the vanity of the human self. At that moment, I felt a release in the core of my being, and I spontaneously said: "God, you can take me home right now."

I had this sense of total surrender, which gave me a feeling of complete inner peace. If I had died at that moment, I could have left the earth behind with no sense of regret and no sense of unfinished business. Amazingly, this total surrender of all ambitions actually was the starting point of discovering my true spiritual mission. I simply had not been able to see this before, as I was still too attached to the vision of my human self and its desire to do something so significant here on earth that God simply had to let the human self into heaven. What an incredible relief to surrender this entire conglomerate of self-created ambitions.

As a result of understanding the importance of surrender and experiencing the freedom of surrender, I had what is no doubt the most life-changing experience yet. During a meditation on divine harmony, I was lifted out of my body and found myself in a spiritual center called the Great Central Sun. This is the seat of Alpha and Omega who are the highest representatives of the Father/Mother God in the world of form. I saw myself standing in this enormous hall, shaped like an amphitheater. There were gigantic columns along the walls and they appeared to be made of solidified light.

I walked down a center aisle until I stood right in front of a throne, upon which sat Alpha and Omega. I saw them as two spheres of white light, and the light was so strong that only their eyes were visible. My attention was drawn to a flow of energy between these two magnificent beings, and I saw it as a horizontal figure-eight flow of liquid light.

I then focused on the nexus of the figure-eight, and as I looked at it, it was as if a portal opened up and I was now looking outside the world of form. Outside was a seemingly endless space that can best be described as a "void," as you find in some religious and mystical teachings. At first, the void appeared empty, but I then became aware that it was not. It was filled with a Being, a Presence, that was conscious yet had no form whatsoever. This being simply *is*.

In a flash, the thought came to me, "This is God!" At that moment, I connected with God, and I knew this was my source; it was from this Being that I came into being. What I experienced was awareness in its purest form. There were no gradations of more or less pure. This awareness simply is. The experience was beyond time and space, and it might have lasted a split second or longer—there was simply no sensation of time or distance. There was no sense of separation, only timeless, boundless oneness. Suddenly, I found myself seated on a cube of white light directly between Alpha and Omega, and I was in the nexus of the figure-eight flow between them.

I experienced a complete peace and a feeling I can only describe as unconditional love. I was experiencing myself as a completely pure self where there was no "space" that could allow for division.

After a time, I noticed that the entire material universe was stretched out before me, and I could see a myriad of galaxies like our Milky Way. Then, my attention was drawn down into this vast space, and I quickly zoomed in on earth, until I came back to my normal state of awareness in my physical body. At the time, this experience was quite earth-shattering to me.

I thought I had a good grip on understanding spiritual teachings, and I felt I had a good intellectual understanding of God. Experiencing the Presence of God was so far beyond any of my paradigms that there was only one thing to do: throw all of my paradigms, expectations and preconceived opinions out the window.

Digesting the experience of the Presence of God

I had experienced the Presence of God, yet there was absolutely no way to describe that Presence through words or images that are intelligible to the human mind. I felt that any attempt to describe God's Presence would be a degradation of that Presence; it would be creating a graven image. I suddenly began to understand why the first two commandments are the first two commandments.

For several years, I told no one about the experience because I needed time to internalize and digest it, but it affected me deeply, and let me describe some of the effects.

I was freed from all desire to think one particular religion was the only true one. I knew no belief system could possibly give a complete description of the Presence of God. That Presence can only be experienced. The best a religion can do is give a description that helps people attain the direct experience, and I began to understand that this is the true purpose behind all spirituality. This gave me an entirely new perspective on spiritual teachings. I saw that if a teaching takes me closer to a direct experience of God's Presence, then it is doing its job regardless of its outer form and doctrines. If it is blocking my direct experience, then the teaching is working against God's intent. The idea that one teaching is the only key to salvation is completely alien to God. I now had a direct proof that I could not sell my soul to one particular church but that I am here for a more universal mission.

I understood that the most important aspect of taking personal responsibility for my spiritual path is that I cannot allow anything to stand between me and God. If I allow a guru or organization or my own human self to stand between me and a direct experience of God, I am worshiping an idol. If I do this, I will never experience the true God who is beyond all idols. God will never fit into my perception filter.

After the experience of being connected to God, all else paled in comparison. Literally, nothing on earth seemed to have the same value to me. It became very clear to me why nothing on this little planet is worth dying for, and with that I mean the death of the soul. The saying "What does it profit a man to gain the whole world yet lose his soul" took on a new meaning. I felt it was worth giving up anything—even physical life—to attain this sense of oneness with God.

God is always within me and we humans have been programmed to limit God's expression through us. It was my foremost job on the spiritual path to undo that programming so I could stop limiting God in me and thereby allow God to do the works through me that God desires to do. I saw that I had to get my human self out of God's way.

In terms of self-esteem, I experienced that God loves me for who I am. God loves the pure self that is an extension of God. I also saw how insignificant is any form of esteem I might gather here on earth compared to the love of God. Even if all people on earth worshipped me as the most important person alive, it would be as nothing compared to the infinite love of

God. I then felt it is far easier to experience the unconditional love of God than to try to set myself up as a god here on earth.

After having digested this experience for a couple of years, it culminated in a real breakthrough. I read something that inspired me to contemplate the question "Why am I here?" I took a walk, sat down in the hills and looked up into the deep, blue sky. I posed the question "Why am I here?" and from deep within my being came the answer: "Because I love God!"

At first this was almost a shock to my outer mind because I had always been trying to understand God, but never quite considered myself as loving God. I now took a closer look at myself. Behind all of the outer personality and beliefs, the bottom line is that I—the real me—truly loves God beyond anything else.

This is simply my basic psychological makeup—an innocent and infinite love for God. I began to see that it is my love for God that brought me to earth. I am here because I love God and because I can see that all other people are God wearing a disguise—they have simply forgotten who they are. I, like many, many other people, volunteered to come here in order to inspire others to discover their true identity and thereby discover their love for God.

Mystical experiences are natural

I know there is a danger in describing this experience because people with low self-esteem will likely feel it is beyond what they could possibly have. My purpose for including it here is to show that ultimate self-esteem comes from knowing we are *all* extensions of God.

The ascended masters have a motto that says: "What one has done, all can do." There is nothing special about me that makes it possible for me to have an experience you can't have.

I started this chapter by talking about mystical experiences and why we cannot force them. The reason is simple. A mystical experience is when the pure self steps outside the perception filter of the human self. Naturally, if we are trying to force this experience in a way that springs from our perception filter, we will not be successful. You cannot escape the mental box of the human self by using the perception of that human self. This is what Jesus called the way that seems right onto a man, but the end of it is the way of death. The Buddha said that if you speak or act with impure perception, suffering follows.

The simple reality is that neither God nor your spiritual self nor the ascended masters are hiding themselves from you. As Jesus said, it is God's good pleasure to give us his kingdom, and God's kingdom is the state of consciousness where we are free from the human perception filter. God also gave us free will, so if we desire to approach God through the human perception filter—seeking to force God to appear to us in the form created by the human self—then God must simply allow us to play this game of creating our own God and worshiping this graven image above the formless God.

If you decide to get serious about questioning your perception filter and invoking spiritual light to transform any accumulated energies in your mind, you will gradually clear the muddy waters. When your mind becomes clear and still, you will naturally have mystical experiences. When I had my first mystical experiences, I saw them as being so different from my normal state of consciousness that I thought they had to be difficult to obtain. I became susceptible to the lie of my human self that having such special experiences required an extraordinary effort.

In reality, having a mystical experience—an experience of oneness with something greater than ourselves—is the natural state of the pure self. What is unnatural is that we see ourselves through the filter of the separate self. Creating and defending this perception filter requires constant effort, and it is this effort that keeps us from having mystical experiences. When we find the spiritual path, we often think that the more we do, the more likely we are to have mystical experiences. The truth is that the more we do with the human self, the more we push away mystical experiences. Instead, what we need to do is to stop doing. We need to stop letting the separate self run our quest for oneness.

When you see and surrender this futile quest of seeking to have the human self guide you to mystical experiences, you will spontaneously start having such experiences. This will create an upward spiral where you will not simply come to understand your true self, but you will experience your self in its purest form. This is not something reserved for the few; it is something all can have. The path I've described in this book can be followed by anyone.

I am not saying your path will be exactly the same as mine or as anyone else's because we are all individuals. By adapting the fundamental insights and steps you've been reading about here to your own life, the path leading towards genuine spiritual experiences will open up for you. And it is through these insights that you can feel the ultimate form of self-esteem that comes only from knowing the self. Knowing the self means experiencing the self in is highest form. And the highest form of your self is the self that is an extension of God—that *is*

God. The path I have described requires work and it takes time. In our modern world, we have all been programmed to want instant gratification. Once you let go of this ego illusion, you'll see that it is worth all the work and surrender to attain the ultimate form of self-worth. Because what could be worth more than *self*-worth?

Keys from Chapter 6

◊ **At a certain stage of the spiritual path** we think the goal is to perfect the human self. This self will never take us beyond the material world.

◊ **The real goal of spiritual growth** is to return to the pure state of the self, which is beyond the distorted perception of the human self.

◊ **Your spiritual teachers and higher self** will give you a frame of reference for knowing what is beyond the perception filter of the human self.

◊ **The human self wants us to think** there are real problems that we need to solve. In reality, we need to surrender the sense that our perception filters show us reality.

◊ **The key to escaping our perception filters** is mystical experiences through which we directly experience a reality outside the human self. We can all have such experiences by clearing away lower energies and illusions.

7 | OVERCOMING GUILT *and* SELF-CONDEMNATION

One of the big obstacles to self-esteem is the fact that most of us have been brought up to feel guilty or to condemn ourselves for any mistake, real or imagined, we have ever made. The major factor that has programmed us to feel bad about our mistakes is the image of an angry and condemning God in the sky. I know most spiritual and New Age people don't actually believe in this God and have probably adopted a view that is closer to my experience of the unconditional God. Yet the angry God is still a very potent image that is used by one aspect of the human self.

Another aspect uses the image of a God who will reward us for living up to the rules defined by a religion here on earth. The human self thinks we will be saved by not doing what the judgmental God says is bad and doing what the rewarding God says is good. In order to develop healthy self-esteem we have to free ourselves from all images of a judgmental God and all images of good and bad.

Before I had my God experience, I had many concepts and mental images about God. I had always sensed that there was something wrong with the standard Christian image of an angry and judgmental being in the sky, but I could never put my finger on it. After this experience, I had to question and surrender any and all images of God in my being. Any time I encountered an image of God from any religious or spiritual teaching, I compared it to my experience. It became my frame of reference for God.

What has been my guide is that the real, true God is a formless and unconditional God and it is a God we can experience directly. For thousands of years people have argued about God, with numerous religious wars as the result. Instead of arguing, it is possible to go beyond our concepts of God and experience the pure Presence of God. Once you have this experience of the unconditional, formless God, your desire to argue about it simply fades away.

If you asked me to describe what God is like, the best answer I would have is: "God is!" If I say anything more than that, we immediately enter the realm of concepts, and concepts are always open to argumentation. Having experienced God, I am not interested in arguing about whether one concept of God is better than another, for I know that no concept or image can encompass the fullness of God. Even saying that God is formless and unconditional is a description in words, and any description in words can be argued against by those who have not had the experience that is beyond words.

It is futile for us to think we can create any spiritual teaching that describes what God is like. It is the human self that wants to take one description of God and elevate it to the status of superiority and infallibility. What we can do is to help people understand the limitations of any image of God, and then help them open themselves to a direct experience of the formless.

The basic fact of life is really quite simple. We live in the world of form. Everything in this world has some kind of shape that sets it apart from other forms. Our minds are so used to dealing with forms that we are unaware of how often we create mental images of something we have not actually experienced—and how we project those images onto other "things" we have not experienced. Unless we go through a process of deliberately deconstructing our mental images, we will tend to think that our mental images are as good as a direct experience of reality—or even that they are reality. We think that projecting an image we have created inside our minds is sufficient for us to know something.

Actually, this is not an unreasonable assumption because there are certain similarities, archetypal forms, in the world of form. For example, there are numerous specific ways to design a table, but if I say the word "table," you instantly have a mental image of what a table is like and what sets it apart from a chair (both of which can have flat tops with four legs).

What does it take to experience God directly? God is beyond form because God is the source of form. If God had a particular form, God could not be the source of all other forms. If God had a definable form, God would also be confined to that form and thus could not be omnipresent and all-powerful. What happens when we take our experiences in the world of form and use them to create a mental image of God and then project it upon the "real thing?" Well, how can any concept based on the world of form give an accurate image of the formless God? By projecting such an image upon

God, and especially when we are firmly convinced that it is accurate, we shut our minds to a direct experience of any reality beyond form. We are more concerned about upholding our mental image than about experiencing a reality that is beyond all possible concepts. Because God is the ultimate respecter of free will, since God gave it to us, God will never force its Presence upon us. God humbly stays hidden behind the form that we insist on making into a graven image and worshiping as our god.

Letting go of guilt

After rethinking my image of God, I started rethinking my images of the world and myself. Once you know that God is formless, you know God is behind, within and the source of all form, and that gives you an entirely different perspective on everything. Among other things, you get a different perspective on guilt and self-condemnation.

Because God is unconditional, God's love is also unconditional. It is not God who wants me to feel guilty for my past choices; it is my human self and the "prince of this world" or the "demons of Mara" who want me to feel guilty. These forces do not want me to look at and change the choices that give them an inroad into my consciousness. It is certain forces in the material world who want to keep me trapped in a lower state of consciousness, whereas God always wants me to move on until I reach the state of consciousness in which I can fully appreciate God's Presence and Being. The formless God does not want me to be trapped in any form but wants me to experience the fullness of its own formless Being and the unconditional love it has for me.

How do I move on so I can experience that love? By making better choices to replace my past choices. In other words, God is not putting any limitations on my growth. God has given me free will. I can make any choice I want, but God does not bind me to my past choices. The purpose of God's creation is to give me an experience in the world of form, and I have this experience by building a certain self. God has no problem with me building any kind of self I decide to create, but God does not want me to remain stuck in that self indefinitely. God wants me to gradually transcend my sense of self until I eventually reach the ultimate form of self-awareness, namely oneness with my Source. I can at any time raise my awareness so I see how a past choice is limiting me. When I see this, I can instantly replace the past choice with a new choice that is not limiting me. This is perfectly acceptable to God, in fact this is how God wants me to react. In contrast, the forces of this world want me to feel that I cannot simply walk away from my past choices, that I need to feel bound by them indefinitely (as in the concept of original sin) or that I need to impose some kind of penance upon myself before I can walk away from them.

Who are these forces that seek to limit me? Well, they are made up of my human self or ego and certain beings who have chosen to enter the consciousness of separation and thus cut themselves off from the spiritual realm. The ascended masters teach that life is a process in which we continually transcend ourselves and move towards higher and higher states of awareness, a higher sense of self. Billions of beings in the material universe have joined this upward or ascending movement, but some beings have chosen to separate themselves from it. Earth is one of the planets where such beings are still allowed to exist. These forces of separation want me to believe that I cannot overcome my past choices through my own power but need an external savior in order to be free. Take note that I am *not* hereby denying karma. We do indeed have to balance the energy (karma) we have generated as a result of past choices, because God has made us responsible for our use of energy. However, by letting go of guilt and transcending our past choices, we can balance the energy much more quickly.

Understanding these truths helped me let go of guilt. I could then begin to look at my past choices and admit "I made a mistake." There is something liberating, almost magical, about admitting that you made a mistake because now the past choice has no more power over you. A mistake that is not admitted cannot be transcended, and in that case you are bound by your past choices. The moment you see the mistake and admit it, you can truly leave the past behind.

What does it take so see a mistake? You need to see at least two options, namely the one you chose and one that is better than what you did. Once you see what is better, there is nothing to stop you from choosing what is better, for the simple fact is that we only made mistakes because we didn't know enough to make a better choice. As the ascended master El Morya, or Master MORE, has said, "If people knew better, they would do better." You cannot come to know better unless you are willing to learn from your mistakes. Once I understood that God does not want me to feel guilty for my mistakes, but the forces of separation do, I decided that I was not going to conform to this manipulation any longer.

It took several years for me to integrate this realization into my life, but the process led me to another groundbreaking conclusion: Nothing I could possibly do would earn me God's love. Nor is there anything I could do that would destroy the love God has for me. The reason is that God's love for me is unconditional. I do not need to live up to any conditions in order to receive it, nor can any conditions keep it from me. God's love is beyond form, and conditions must have some kind of form. Unless there is a specific form, how can you determine whether I live up to a condition or fail to do so? Conditions can exist only in a realm lower than the formless God.

I have already earned God's love by the fact that God created me. I am worthy of God's love because God created me worthy. When it comes to God's love, I only have two options: I can accept it or I can reject it. How can I reject it? Only by defining a condition and then perceiving that I do not live up to it and thus am not worthy of God's love.

What is self-condemnation?

On the spiritual path everything is a gradual process. In other words, I had an amazing experience of God's Presence, but afterwards I was returned to my old sense of self. I did have a new frame of reference that provided me with a radically different perspective, but my old sense of self was not instantly gone. It took quite a lot of processing and breakthrough experiences for me to fully let go of the old self.

This point is beautifully described by Marianne Williamson in *A Return to Love*. She describes how she had her moment of surrender where she asked God for help, but then she went through a very turbulent period and it took several years before she found a new equilibrium. I have experienced the exact same thing several times in my life. When we break through and sincerely reach out for deliverance, we will indeed receive deliverance. However, what we often don't realize is that the deliverance comes in the form of an injection of spiritual light that flushes out all of the unresolved stuff in our subconscious minds. When I experienced God's Presence, I received light that started flushing out all of my unresolved stuff concerning my relationship with God. Your path will be different, but rethinking your view of God can't be done overnight. It will likely take some time for you to process these subtle concepts and overcome your illusions about who God is and who you are.

We were all brought up with a limited understanding of both God and the self, which causes us to have a lack of self-worth. A lack of something might sound like a passive measure, but ignorance is actually a very active measure. Ignorance comes because we have limiting beliefs in our perception filters. These beliefs are not sitting there passively; they are actively and aggressively projecting a mental image upon us, the world and God. Human *perception* is actually human *projection*. Our lives are so easily eaten up by trying to justify the illusions of the human self rather than discovering the reality of the spiritual self.

Low self-worth is a very active process where we are constantly projecting a degrading image upon ourselves. Our lack of self-esteem tricks us into seeking self-worth through something in this world. The subtle mechanism behind this is that everything in this world has form. This means you can compare one form to another based on their differences. What our human selves do is to impose a value judgment on top of this comparison process. The human self operates with a scale, and it has good at one end and bad on the other end.

If you look at this planet as a whole, you can see that different civilizations can have different scales for defining what is good or bad, and this is my point. As long as you seek to get self-esteem by living up to certain conditions (that are defined as good) and avoiding other conditions (defined as bad), you will never have true self-esteem. Instead, you will be bound to a treadmill of always having to evaluate yourself based on this relative value judgment.

What that means is very simple. If you do live up to your relative conditions, you can feel secure or you might even feel pride because you are so good or spiritual. If you do not live up to these conditions, you automatically end up feeling bad about yourself, likely condemning yourself for not measuring up to the standard. Both superiority and inferiority keep you from experiencing the self in its pure state.

As long as we believe in this relative value judgment, we are trapped in seeking to live up to a standard defined in this world. We are constantly projecting upon ourselves a mental image based on the value judgment of good and bad, yet both are defined by our human selves and thus degrade who we really are. We are essentially projecting the image that we are less than the pure being God created. In reality, this is a form of spiritual pride because we think we have the right to judge what God created in unconditionality.

As long as we judge like this, we will not be able to move on to the higher level of finding true self-esteem by experiencing the self in its formless state. For many years I was focused on living up to outer conditions defined by a spiritual teaching and movement. In fact, it's even possible to use a spiritual teaching to intensify our self-condemnation. A spiritual teaching always sets up a high goal, so as long as you have not attained cosmic consciousness or freedom from sin, one part of your self has the perfect justification for condemning the totality of self.

The self that generates self-condemnation

It was only my experience of God as being formless that empowered me to start the process whereby I eventually came to see through this entire self-destructive state of consciousness. But what kind of self was able to experience the formless God?

Right after I had that experience, I was not consciously aware of how challenging it had been, not only to my view of God but to my view of myself. In retrospect, I see that when you experience the formless God, you also have a frame of reference for evaluating yourself. My human sense of self simply could not have withstood the experience of the formless God. The experience of the formless is indeed the ultimate challenge to the self that is based on form. It also helps us see that we are more than the form-based self.

It took me over 10 years of processing my experience to reach the point where I could receive the teaching about the pure self, or what the ascended masters call the Conscious You. The essence of this teaching is that the core of my self is a being that came from the spiritual realm, and thus it has no form as form is defined in the material world. It did not come from dust and will not return to dust. It came from the formless God, and it has the potential to return to oneness with that God. The importance of this teaching cannot be overstated.

It helped me go through a process of coming to see that my "self" is by no means a homogenous whole. I already knew this intellectually, because I had been aware of teachings about the human self or ego since the 1980s. Intellectual understanding is not the same as experiencing the reality of something. What happened during my experience of God's Presence was that I also experienced myself as a formless self, which helped me come to see that the rest of my sense of self was based on form and that there are specific aspects of this form-based self.

For example, look at how we are brought up to see ourselves as playing various roles in the theater of life. We are first supposed to be good children, good students, good employees, good spouses, good parents and so on. There isn't necessarily anything limiting in this, but depending on how these roles are defined in our particular family and society, they may indeed be very limiting to our creative expression and the fulfillment of our divine plans. These roles are all defined in order to get us to conform to external expectations and they might leave very little room for bringing forth creativity from within ourselves. Just look at how many women were brought up to play the role of second-class citizens who were supposed to accept that they had nothing to contribute to society besides bringing forth children and satisfying the sexual desires of their husbands.

I started seeing the impact of roles in my early teens when I distributed newspapers in an upper middle-class neighborhood. I knew I could go to college and get everything these people had and I knew this was what my working-class parents wanted for me. I also knew that this simply would not be a fulfilling life for me and that I was meant to find a different, more spiritual approach to life.

The teachings of the ascended masters and my inner guidance helped me get a clearer picture that my life has a spiritual purpose, what the masters call our divine plan. This also helped me expose my human self, and as soon as I saw an aspect of my human self, I knew that this was not truly who I am. I could then mentally step outside of this form-based self, see it from the outside and see that it was not the real me. This process makes it so much easier to let go of the human self; in fact it makes it effortless. Because every time you let go of some aspect of the human self, you feel freer than before.

How we define mistakes

Many spiritual people have a hard time accepting that there are forces who seek to destroy our spiritual growth. For example, Irene was a very gentle soul who believed that if she did not harm any form of life, God would not allow anything to harm her. She once told me that she had trouble sleeping because she had so many thoughts coming to her mind. I told her that I used to have the same problem until I learned to invoke spiritual light from Archangel Michael for protection and from Elohim Astrea to be cut free from dark forces. As soon as I said "dark forces," Irene looked at me as if I was radioactive and she couldn't get away fast enough.

Regardless of how you see it, I think all spiritual people have experienced that there is something outside of us, whether you call it a dark force or something else, that projects the feeling of guilt and blame into our minds. We get a sense that we have done something so bad that we can never make up for it. That is very much tied into the false idea that we have committed such a grave sin that God has rejected us and there is nothing we ourselves can do to make up for it. This feeling is what forms a closed mental box, a catch-22, because if you fear that admitting a mistake will condemn you to an eternity in hell, you will resist admitting the mistake.

Even though it is necessary for us to admit that we made a mistake, it is also important to realize that we only made the mistake because we were looking at the situation through the limited and distorted perception of the human self. If our perception had been pure, we would have seen the situation differently and thus would not have made the mistake. If we had known better, we would have done better.

Even though you may have made certain mistakes, it was not the *real* you who did this. It was the human self, and you are not your human self. Whenever I would feel these heavy projections of guilt and condemnation, I would use the mantra: "Yes, I did it, but it was not the real me who did it."

You may say this sounds like I was refusing to take responsibility by denying that I did it, but the reality is more subtle. I did admit that I had made a mistake and then saw that it was because my view of the situation had been colored by my human self. I then used the situation to separate myself from that human self so that I could turn the situation into a forward step on my path. I was moving one step closer to oneness rather than having the situation keeping me trapped in separation.

Sometimes people on the spiritual path can be very judgmental or critical towards others. For example, James was very particular about following all of the rules of his spiritual organization and he clearly looked down upon those who were not as diligent as he was. Over the years I knew James, he began to find it harder and harder to keep up his zeal. He was trapped by a simple mechanism.

If James had started to relax on following the rules, he would have had to judge himself as harshly as he had judged others. He simply could not bear to have his own judgmental attitude directed at himself, so he had to keep up the outer behavior even though it was clearly not helping him grow and was only making him miserable.

This is actually the deeper meaning of Jesus' saying to do unto others as we want them to do unto us. What we do to others can, in actuality, tell us something about what we do to ourselves at subconscious levels. If you are very critical towards others, it shows that at subconscious levels you are equally critical of yourself. In order to do something to others, you must first have done the same thing to yourself at subconscious levels.

The reason for that is that you have an aspect of the human self that is designed to judge everyone based on a human standard and you will inevitably judge yourself by the same standard. Of course, you can't handle being judged so harshly, so you have created another aspect of the human self to deflect that judgment towards others so you can live with yourself. The price you pay is that you constantly have to live up to your standard in order to avoid the judging finger pointing at you—and this takes the joy out of life.

In essence, we use one aspect of our human self to deal with another aspect, but this can never end with one aspect winning over the other. It can only end when we become aware of both aspects and decide to abandon both of them. That is why the human self simply has to die. The human self gives us the impression that there is a problem to be solved, such as a need to judge others by a certain standard. James thought that if he could get other people to follow the spiritual teachings he believed in, it would solve all of the world's problems. The real enigma to be solved, however, is to see how two aspects of the human self are simply keeping each other alive by keeping us trapped in a perpetual struggle.

This principle has helped me resolve many situations. I went through a period in my life where I was feeling a lot of projections about being guilty of this, that and the next thing. There was simply no end to what I was supposed to feel guilty about. I finally used the technique of repeating a mantra every time I felt a projection of guilt: "There is nothing wrong with me." What this did for me was to reconnect me to the fact that I was created as a pure spiritual being and regardless of what I might have done through the human self, there is nothing wrong with the pure being that God created—and I am still that being.

One might also say that my unworthy self was projecting guilt at me, but instead of defending myself through the worthy self, I used the projection to affirm that I am more than both aspects of my human self. I learned that I could turn the very projection that was meant to keep me trapped in my human self into a tool to help me separate myself from the human self.

How to change your past

We can actually take this one step further. Guilt is usually tied to an action we have taken in the material world or to the consequences of an action. The essential characteristic of the material world is that time moves in only one direction. We can never undo what we have done in the past. We can't turn back the clock so there seems to be no way to escape the guilt of having made a mistake—or so the human self wants us to believe.

The human self will always have two polarities. It is therefore inevitable that we will sometimes act through the one polarity (the unworthy self) that makes us do what the other polarity (the worthy self) labels as a mistake. The human self will then attempt to make us believe that we should feel guilty for this mistake forever because there is no way to change what was done in the past.

Here's the key: not only are the past actions we've taken based on the perception filter of the human self, but our reaction to the situation was also based on human perception. This perception, however, is not ultimately real; it exists largely in our own mind and in the collective consciousness. As long as we act based on the human self and react to our actions based on the human self, the inevitable consequence is that we keep ourselves trapped in the slavery of the human self.

How can we escape this never-ending cycle of action and reaction? It takes a different approach to life, and it has more than one component. The first component is to acknowledge that the purpose of life on earth has very little to do with the actual physical circumstances we experience, including the choices we make and their physical consequences. The teachings of the ascended masters make it clear that the material universe is a learning environment, a kind of laboratory in which we can experiment with our creative abilities. The purpose is not to produce a particular physical outcome; the deeper purpose is to help us raise our consciousness, to expand our self-awareness.

The all-important consequence of this view is that in any situation we encounter on earth, the important thing is not the physical outcome *but the effect that the situation has on our state of consciousness*. The material world is like a sandbox. Nothing here is permanent and whatever we do is like building a sand castle because everything is done with energy and no form will last forever. No matter how big of a castle we build, the sand can always be returned to its undifferentiated state.

How to move on with life

The second component is based on a simple fact that I think all who believe in reincarnation can accept. No matter how severe a mistake you have made, you will not live forever in your current physical body. When your body dies, you may come back in another lifetime, but you will not remember what you did in the past.

This forgetting demonstrates that God and our spiritual teachers do not want us to forever be burdened by mistakes made in the past. They only want us to learn our lessons and then move on. What is the lesson? It is that acting through the human self will always produce undesirable consequences and make us feel bad about ourselves. The real mistake we made is not that we took some physical action. The real mistake we made is that we took action based on the distorted perception of the human self and then we reacted based on the human self.

Regardless of the physical consequences of any action we might take, the mistake is not the action or its consequences. The initial mistake was to act through the human self, and if we allow the human self to make us feel guilty about it, we are only compounding the mistake. We are upholding the distorted perception of the human self, and this will inevitably cause us to make more mistakes in a spiral that will never end—until we say stop.

I have felt only unconditional love from God and I know that no matter what I have done on earth, God loves me with a love that is beyond any conditions defined on earth. God only wants us to grow into a state of oneness with our Source and with each other. This growth towards oneness simply cannot happen through the human self. This brings me to the third component.

Let's say I killed someone 10 lifetimes ago. How can you kill another human being? Well, in reality the pure you cannot kill a human being because you can kill only what you see as different from yourself. Of course, the human self sees every other person as different from itself and that is why the human self can believe in a very persuasive lie: I can harm you without that affecting me. I can get away with things. Just look at how many criminals believe that if they can avoid being caught by the police, they have gotten away with a crime and then there will be no further consequences.

As spiritual people who believe in karma and reincarnation, we know that we can never get away with anything. We will be responsible for our actions and our use of energy, and the karma will follow us until we do something to balance it. This is one important motivation for performing spiritual exercises, and the ascended masters make it clear that invoking spiritual light is the most efficient way to balance karma. The masters also teach that invoking spiritual light only balances the energy side of the karma equation. The other side of the equation is that we have to transcend the consciousness that caused us to make certain mistakes. Let's dissect a mistake so you can see what I mean. Again, say I killed someone 10 lifetimes ago.

The action created an energy impulse that was sent out into the four levels of the material universe. At some point, the energy will return to me at the physical level, and it might indeed have the effect that I will be killed.

However, this is not done as the punishment of an angry God; it is done in order to give me a second opportunity to learn my lesson. What was my first opportunity to learn? It was to evaluate my action and my reaction to it. Why did I kill that person 10 lifetimes ago? Because I had become so blinded by my human self that I felt threatened by the other person and I thought killing the person was a viable, perhaps even a justifiable, way out. So how did I react to the situation? Well, I had two basic options.

The most common reaction would be to react through my human self, the very self that caused me to kill the person. This might cause me to react either by seeking to justify my action or by feeling deep guilt because of what I did. Beyond that, I had an option that is not normally recognized by people. That option is to see that my action was based on the flawed perception of my human self.

I could then decide to consciously seek to rise above that perception by raising my consciousness. I could recognize that my mistake was based on the illusion that I am a separate being and I could make an effort to move back to oneness. This is essentially what every true spiritual teaching has attempted to teach us, from the Buddha's teachings and the *Tao Te Ching* to Jesus' teachings about turning the other cheek.

Is sin an illusion?

What is the purpose of life on earth? It is that we have experiences that help us expand our sense of self. What is the logical consequence of expanding our sense of self? It is that our sense of self encompasses more and more until we realize the underlying reality that all life is one and sprang from the same source.

In my experience, those of us who grew up in a Christian culture have been deeply affected by a world view that says that some of the things we can do on earth are wrong in some absolute way. God gave us free will because it is only by making choices and experiencing the consequences that we grow. The only way to give us a will that is truly free is to give us the option to go into the consciousness of separation where we might deny our oneness with God. There is no law saying that we have to go into separation, but if we desire to have the experience of seeing the world through a separate self, then God's law of free will allows us to do this.

By giving us this freedom, God knew it was taking a calculated risk. The effect of the consciousness of separation is that it creates a perception filter that is out of touch with reality. And once we look at the world from inside the filter, we will be convinced that what we see is indeed reality. Once we are inside the mental box, there is seemingly no way out of the box.

God knew this and that is why the world is designed with a subtle safety mechanism. The reality of God is oneness. How do we leave oneness and go into separation? We can leave oneness only by dividing into at least two forms that are seen as opposites. That is why the human self will always have two

polarities. The consequence is that once we step into the consciousness of separation and create the first division of the
human self, we will not be able to stop the fragmentation of
the separate self.

Taking an action based on the duality of the human self
will inevitably lead to two opposite reactions, such as the worthy and the unworthy self. We will experience our action and
its consequences through the two aspects of the human self
and that is why we can never be at peace with any action taken
through the human self.

We will likely take further actions through one aspect of the
human self. This will lead to more undesirable consequences
and we will again respond by creating a further division. Pretty
soon the human self is divided into so many contradictory
parts that our entire waking consciousness is eaten up in a
seemingly never-ending action-reaction sequence.

The only way out is to become conscious of this process and decide to no longer react based on the human self.
Instead, we must find a way to break the human action-
reaction sequence. This is what the Buddha attempted to help
us do with his concept that everything is created in pairs and
that we are the products of our past thoughts. It is what Jesus
attempted to help us do with his teachings about letting the
human self die and by turning the other cheek.

Consider the profound truth behind the teaching to turn
the other cheek. Let's say someone slaps me on one cheek.
What is the typical reaction of the human self? It is to either
seek to get away (flight) or to hit the person back (fight). The
deeper understanding of Jesus' teaching is that turning the
other cheek means we neither flee nor fight back. Instead,
we remain completely neutral and give the person another

opportunity to hit us. What is the purpose in that? To help us break the sequence of reacting to every situation through the duality of the human self. If you can turn the other cheek, you have made great strides towards escaping the blindness of the human self.

Let me return to the idea that I cannot change the "fact" that I killed someone 10 lifetimes ago. This is true; however, what affects me today is not what I did 10 lifetimes ago but how I allowed the action and its consequences to affect my state of consciousness.

I had two options at that time. One is that I could have reacted to my action through the human self, thus building deeper and deeper layers of division of that human self. This means that every action I take today happens through those layers of my human perception filter. For instance, I might have justified my actions of killing someone and therefore built layers of justification causing me to be a criminal or a psychopath in this lifetime. Or I might have felt guilt, causing me to feel bad about myself and spend lifetimes seeking to compensate for what I did in the past.

The alternative is that I could have used my unbalanced action as a way to become more conscious of my human self and then used the situation to separate myself from that human self. This is exactly what God and my spiritual teachers want me to do. Whether I deny my former mistakes or feel guilty about them, I am still trapped in the human self. But God only wants me to start separating myself from the human self so I can move into oneness.

In effect, it's not constructive to continue to feel guilt over my mistakes. In order to overcome a mistake, I need to accomplish three things:

- If the mistake had physical consequences that still affect me and other people, I need to take appropriate actions to deal with those consequences.

- I need to invoke spiritual light in order to transform the energy that I misqualified as a result of my actions.

- I need to make a conscious effort to rise above the aspect of the human self that caused me to make the mistake.

Once I have done these things—the last one being the most important—I have no need to feel guilt. In fact, *I cannot rise above the consciousness that caused me to make the mistake as long as I feel guilty about it.* That's because it was one aspect of my human self that caused me to make the mistake and the opposite polarity of the human self that caused me to feel guilty about it. Both aspects must be transcended before I am free of the consciousness that caused the mistake.

As long as we are afraid that admitting a mistake will plunge us into unbearable guilt, it is almost impossible to admit a mistake. Once we see that we can acknowledge our mistakes without feeling the guilt, we can progress much faster on the path to oneness. When I finally understood this truth, it was as if the demons of guilt had lost their power over me and my path became so much easier.

The mechanics of self-condemnation

We can't have real self-esteem if we constantly feel guilty and critical of ourselves. Perhaps what I've said so far about guilt has helped you see why guilt is unnecessary. I'd like to share some further thoughts on this from a different angle. Though this may feel as if I am repeating myself a bit, bear with me, because I've found that it can be very difficult for people, including myself, to understand the full implications of this point.

Let's consider a simple question: How is it even possible for us to condemn ourselves? Which part of the self is capable of condemning the self? Once we have some experience of pure awareness, of a formless state of consciousness, we can easily see the answer. In the unconditional love and oneness of God, condemnation is simply impossible. Condemnation means that something is condemning something else. Since there is no division in God, how can there be one part acting upon another part? Condemnation is possible only in the realm of separation. This means that it is not the pure self that feels condemnation for itself. The pure self is created out of God's Being, and how could God condemn an extension of itself? Once again, we can experience self-condemnation only because we are looking through a perception filter, a filter defined by the human self.

When we are looking through this filter, the form-based standard seems absolutely real and necessary, as does the value judgment imposed by the human self. It seems real to us that in order to attain self-esteem, we must create a self based on this relative standard, a self that lives up to the conditions defined as good.

Taoism and Buddhism teach that the two dualistic polarities are inseparable. Once we go into this dualistic state of mind, we think we must run towards one extreme and run away from the opposite extreme. Now think about something we all learned in elementary school, namely the concept of action and reaction. For every action, there is an opposite and equal reaction.

When we are seeking to run towards what we see as good, we are creating an action. By natural law, our action must have an opposite and equal reaction from the universe. We might consciously think that we are trying to create a self that is good and spiritual but it is inevitable that our efforts to create this unbalanced self will generate an opposite reaction. In other words, at the very same time we are creating a good self, we will also be creating a bad self.

The formless self that we are is now caught in the middle; it is in a tug-of-war between two aspects of the human self. The good self is trying to pull us towards one extreme and the bad self is trying to pull us towards the other extreme. The struggle between them eats up our conscious attention so we never have a quiet moment to consider whether there is more to life. We can escape this chaos by realizing that we are not actually condemning ourselves. It is simply the worthy self condemning the unworthy self while the real "me" is the formless self, the pure self.

As a visual example, consider that you are floating in a river. You try to swim towards one bank but in the middle of the river is an anchor and you are tied to it with a bungee cord. As you swim towards one shore, you pull the bungee cord tighter and tighter. Eventually you have created such a tension in the cord that you cannot swim against it and you are pulled towards the other shore. You can continue swimming towards one or the other shore until you are completely exhausted and realize that you don't want to do this any more. At that point you can surrender the struggle and simply flow with the river of life.

This is another example of a catch-22. We have probably all experienced that there are opposite forces in our psyches. We may not be fully conscious of what they are, but we feel the opposite pulls on us. At the same time, most of us have been brought up with a spiritual or religious teaching that says God will accept us only when we live up to certain conditions defined here on earth.

We now have a self that is constantly seeking to pull us towards living up to these conditions, and we have another self that is pulling us towards the opposite extreme—with equal force. The bad self does not want to be restricted by anything, so the good self is seeking to make us feel so bad that we will obey it in order to escape its constant condemnation. Seemingly, there is only one way out: We must redouble our efforts to meet the standard so the good self can win over the bad self.

The good self, however, can *never* win over the bad self because for every action there is an opposite and equal reaction. No matter how much effort I expend in seeking to be good, my very efforts will generate an opposite reaction from the universe. In other words, I may be seeking to pull myself towards being good, but the universe itself, by God's design, pulls me towards the opposite. The harder I pull in one direction, the harder the universe will pull me back.

What kind of a twisted divine mind would come up with this scenario? Well, a formless mind, of course. God is formless and it has sent an extension of itself into the world of form. God wants the pure self to experience the world of form from the inside. We experience this world through the perception filter of a specific form-based self. The world seems real because we are fully identified with this self, having forgotten our formless aspect. There is nothing wrong with us doing this and God has given us free will to have any experience we want for as long as we want. We grow by going through the process of forgetting and reawakening.

Now consider this. If stepping into a form-based self makes the world of form seem absolutely real, how can the pure self ever rise above this identification with form and come back to knowing that it came from the formless? The action-reaction scenario is a cosmic safety mechanism built into the design of the universe. We create a form-based self by using a relative scale with two polarities. However, we can create two forms of form-based self:

- A self that is connected to something greater than itself. This is a self that has not gone into the illusion of separation and duality. It knows it is part of something greater than itself and thus it is expanding its sense of self based on this sense of connectedness.

- A separate self, which thinks it is self-existing and has the right to define good and evil. This is a self based on the illusion of separation, which must have a division into dualistic opposites. This self is seeking to expand its sense of power by using the consciousness of duality in which it can justify all of its actions. It has become a closed system.

For the connected self, the two creative polarities are complementary; but for the separate self, they are opposites. This means that a separate self is created out of a fundamental division. As we move towards one extreme, we create an opposite force that seeks to pull us back towards the center. We have a perfect right to experience the world through the perception filter of a separate self. Because this type of self makes separation seem real, there has to be a mechanism that can allow us to return to formlessness. Otherwise we might be trapped in this separate self indefinitely, and why would a formless God want an extension of itself to be trapped in form forever?

The built-in safety mechanism is that when we enter into a separate self, everything we do creates an opposite reaction, which makes life a constant struggle. This is what the Buddha described as the first noble truth, namely that when you are trapped in duality, everything is a struggle.

Problems with no solutions

What makes this a catch-22 is that once we experience life through the perception filter of a separate self, we think it shows us a real problem that has to be solved. The problem is not a real problem: it is a perceived problem that exists only in the mental box of the human self. The only real solution is to see through the illusion that created the appearance that there was a problem.

Let's look at the problem of self-esteem. A separate self can never have true self-esteem. The reason is that the separate self is never one self; it is always a divided self. One aspect of this self pulls you in one direction and the other pulls you in the opposite direction, so you can never live up to the relative standard.

Of course, we don't usually see these contradictory forces clearly but experience ourselves as one self. Because we also feel the opposites pull on us, we bind ourselves to the process of seeking self-esteem from the outside. Our experience is that we cannot get it from inside the self—the reason being the contradictory forces of self—so we have to look for it somewhere else.

I have seen people in spiritual movements, and I went through it myself, have the sense that because of all the outer things they had done for their movement, they were truly spiritual. In every spiritual movement I have seen, you can see people who have attained a position in the organization, who have been members for a long time or who have made large financial contributions, and they often act as if this entitles them to special status.

Jane, for example, had been largely responsible for building up a specific spiritual organization in Denmark. She thought this gave her the right to demand strict discipline and obedience from others and to treat them very harshly if they did not obey her. Philip, an old friend of mine, calls this the "mini guru syndrome" because such people often try to set themselves up as having the same unquestionable status as the leader of their organizations. It is a disease that affects most spiritual movements (and most religious, business, scientific and political organizations as well).

Jane basically thought she was the guru's only representative in Denmark and that all the rest of us should treat her as such, even when she exposed us to obvious ego-based behavior. Her abusive behavior was eventually reported to the organization's headquarters in America, and Jane was given a mild discipline. This was such a blow to her pride that she could never again relate to the people who had reported her and she basically dropped out of the organization. There are plenty of examples of people who had the same experience and, as a result, they turned against their former teacher, making all kinds of unsubstantiated claims against him or her. My purpose for describing this mechanism is to show that the contradictory aspects of the separate self will never allow us to build self-esteem based on an outer standard. Many spiritual people actually sense this without being consciously aware of it. That is what puts us into this mode of looking for some miraculous outer event, such as finding the perfect guru who can take us out of this bind. We are looking for something from outside the self to do for us what we sense the self cannot do by itself.

The self can indeed free itself, but it will never do this by seeking to solve the problem defined by the separate self. We will be free only by coming to see that this problem is entirely unreal, and thus our struggle is entirely self-created. If the problem is self-condemnation, the central issue is that the human self believes it has to live up to a standard in this world. One aspect of the human self is constantly condemning us because in the past we were not perfect according to some standard. Another aspect of the human self is frantically seeking to deal with this by either denying it, by doing something to compensate for it or by doing something so spiritual that the old mistakes won't matter. It may even try to create a new standard to convince us that what we did was not bad at all.

What we have created, we can also uncreate. How do we overcome the separate self? By coming to see that the two aspects of the human self are created at the same time and one cannot exist without the other. These two selves will be locked in a battle for the indefinite future because they are like computers that cannot go beyond their programming. They do what they do because that is all they can do. So it really is a matter of how long we will allow ourselves to be on this seesaw.

Escaping the human duality

The human self cannot see its own limitations and it cannot see that ultimately its struggle is unreal and has no consequence. It will think the problem is real and that solving it has epic importance, perhaps even that it is doing this for God. The pure self can see the unreality of this mechanism and it can recognize that our attention is being pulled into this senseless struggle and can stay there for lifetimes. The only way out of the catch-22 is to simply walk away from this pointless struggle by giving up trying to solve the problem that the separate self has defined.

How do we walk away from the struggle? By returning to the state of pure awareness where we acknowledge one simple truth: God has not defined any conditions that we have to live up to in order to receive God's esteem. We are worthy of God's esteem by the very fact that God created us. The form-based self can never be worthy of God's esteem. The only way for the pure self to experience God's esteem is to go through the ultimate surrender of letting go of the separate self and returning to the state of pure, formless awareness. It is only in pure awareness that we will experience the unconditional love that God has for us.

Keys from Chapter 7

◊   **God or our spiritual teachers** have no desire for us to feel guilty; they only want us to transcend the human self.

◊   **Self-condemnation** is possible only because the human self is always divided. One aspect of the human self makes us do something and another aspect of the human self condemns us for having done it.

◊   In reality, **the pure self did not make a mistake**. It simply acted based on the flawed perception of the human self. Thus, every mistake can be used to expose the human self and transcend our perception filters.

◊   **The key to spiritual growth** is to take command over your reaction to anything you encounter in the world so you don't react through the human self.

◊   **One aspect of the human self** is constantly saying you are unworthy. Another aspect is saying you can become worthy by living up to a standard defined on earth. In reality, the worthy self cannot exist without the unworthy self, so you can never escape the tension between self-condemnation and self-justification.

◊   **Your higher self** and spiritual teachers will help you gradually see through and then surrender the human duality so that you can see with pure perception.

8 | ATTAINING UNCONDITIONAL SELF-ESTEEM

Even for those who have studied spiritual teachings for a long time, it is difficult to deal with unconditional love. This is, of course, no wonder since the world programs us to believe that love can only be conditional. Here's a typical example. Jennifer had a very controlling mother and a very submissive father. She felt her mother was trying to control her by withholding love and affection and she felt her father never supported her in dealing with her mother. She therefore grew up feeling that any expression of love was dependent on her living up to conditions that were only restricting her freedom.

Jennifer was also deeply affected by her Christian church and the image of an angry and judgmental God. Even though she has been following the teachings of the ascended masters for decades, Jennifer still holds on to the image of the angry God and even projects that the ascended masters are judgmental and take sides in personal disputes. When I tried to tell her about my experience of unconditional love, she flat out rejected it and argued that I had experienced a false God. She had elaborate intellectual arguments for why God could not possibly love us unconditionally and why we had to live up to conditions in order to be worthy of God's love. There was no way we could be worthy of God's love by the nature of who we are, she said.

Such attitudes are not surprising because most of us grew up experiencing only conditional love from parents, teachers and spouses who all wanted us to live up to certain conditions before they gave us love. We are brainwashed into thinking love is something we can get only when we deserve it. This is, of course, the way it often is here on earth, but is it true for God also?

When I had the experience of the formless God, I did not recognize that what I was feeling from God was love. That's because my experience of love up to that point had been conditional, or human, love. The experience of God, and the feeling it gave me, was so different that for years I did not associate that experience with love. I was hesitant to put any words to it, especially the word love, because what I had felt was so pure that I did not want it associated with the concept of human love.

A few years after the experience, I was prompted to contemplate the idea: If God's love is unconditional, what conditions could I possibly have to fulfill in order to receive God's love? If there are any conditions to fulfill, then God's love is not truly unconditional, is it? The only condition I have to fulfill is to overcome the illusion that I have to live up to any conditions! If I am not receiving God's love, it is not because God isn't giving it to me.

It is because I am actively rejecting it by thinking I am not worthy of it (because I do not live up to this or that standard).

If I am rejecting God's love, I am in a very real sense reject-ing God. I am in effect saying that I know better than God whether or not I am worthy.

When I experienced the Presence of God, I felt a flow of energy from God to me, and I finally acknowledged that this was love—only it was a love so completely different from human love that there is no comparison. Given that I could find no other word, I started calling it "unconditional love." In reality, there are no words that can convey the experience.

Because I acknowledged that what I had felt was God's love for me, I began opening my mind to the possibility of experiencing it again. After a while, I began having glimpses of the feeling. Sometimes it would be for only a split second and with less strength than the original feeling.

Other times I would lie half-awake for a long time bathed in the feeling of unconditional love. Today I simply need to still my outer mind in order to feel this love as a background experience for everything else. It is there constantly, but it is difficult to maintain a clear awareness of it during daily activ-ities. Again, I know there is a danger in describing my experi-ence because it might make people think that since they haven't had a similar or a similarly dramatic experience, there must be something wrong with them. I am describing the experience because I know that many spiritual seekers have had at least some glimpses of unconditionality—an experience that there is something outside our normal mental box or life experience. Although you may not have associated this experience with love (or even recognized it as something out of the ordinary), any experience of the unconditional can be used as a stepping stone for opening your mind to unconditional love. Look back at your life and consider whether you have had any experiences of a different state of consciousness. It might have been a sense of expanded awareness, of witnessing yourself from the outside, of being connected to something greater, of inner peace. Or a sense of having dreamt or experienced a situation before it happened, a sense of recognizing another person or recognizing a statement as truth.

These experiences come from the intuitive part of your mind, the part that is beyond the human self. Whereas the intellect wants to divide reality into parts so that it can analyze and categorize them, intuition looks at the whole. It is through this faculty that we can experience something beyond the normal mental box created by the intellect, the linear, analytical mind that is the primary tool the human self uses to gain a sense of being in control of life.

Why the human self rejects love

God's unconditional love is being offered to all of us constantly. So if you are not experiencing unconditional love from God, it is simply because you are rejecting it. Why do some of us reject unconditional love? What advantages do we (or to be more specific, our human selves) gain from rejecting unconditional love?

To understand that, we have to build on the idea that if we want to raise our awareness, we have to completely transcend the human consciousness in which we see ourselves as separate beings. The human self was born out of the illusion of separation, and thus if we overcome that illusion, the human self will gradually lose power over us until it literally shrivels up and dies. Since the human self does not want to die, the human self will always resist our attempts to overcome the illusion of separation. The most powerful tool it has for accomplishing this goal is to get us to reject unconditional love.

The ego doesn't want us to accept unconditional love because once we experience it we realize it is the great unifier. Love—that is, unconditional love, not human love—is literally the driving force behind the cosmos. It is the basic force that drives God to create and that drives all life to self-transcend and come closer to oneness with God. As we experience this, we will begin to see that there is no barrier between us and God because God has no desire whatsoever to keep its love from us. As Jesus says, "it is the father's good pleasure to give you the kingdom."

Once we begin to see this, we also begin to see through the fundamental illusion that allows the human self and the dark forces to exist. This illusion is that "reality" can be divided into two spheres: One is what we experience on earth—where we do not have God's love—and the other is a paradise in which we would be bathed in God's love but from which we are separated by an impenetrable barrier. The illusion says that God created this division and that God has defined the conditions that caused us to be thrown out of paradise and that will allow us, if we meet them, to get back into heaven (in some distant place and time).

Once you begin to experience unconditional love, you see that this is a complete and utter lie. In reality, it is not God who created the division because in God there is no division. God is beyond form, so God has no internal parts that can be separated by a barrier. God is unconditional, so how can God define conditions that apply only to some extensions of itself? God is omnipresent, so how can we find a place where God is not? Beings with free will created the division and it exists only in our minds. We created the division because it gives us the opportunity to experience what it is like to be separate beings—as opposed to beings who are part of a greater whole.

There are things we can experience and do as separate beings that we cannot experience as part of the whole. When we see ourselves as separate beings, we have divided humanity into two groups: ourselves and the others. We can now play that ancient game of "us versus them." For example, we cannot experience being better or being more important than others when we realize that all other self-aware beings also came from God and are loved unconditionally by God. Likewise, we cannot control other people if we believe we are all part of the same unit. And we cannot "do unto others" if we know that what we do unto others we are also doing to ourselves— because there are no others.

God has given us the right to experience life through the filter of separation. What prevents us from being stuck in separation forever is that separation can only be created through a division into two opposites. The tension between the opposites makes our lives filled with suffering and prevents us from being at peace. It is simply a matter of how much suffering we have to experience before we decide we have had enough of separation and want to return to oneness. We return to oneness by questioning the perception filter of the separate self, including its view of love.

In unconditional love, there is no room for saying some people are loved more than others. Unconditional love is no respecter of persons. In order to maintain the illusion that we are more important than others, we must create the sense of division, which then gives rise to conditions. Only then can we say that those who do not meet certain conditions are bad or are not loved by God. The only problem with that line of reasoning is that it does not apply to the real God. It applies only to a conditional god, a god that we have created by defining a mental image and projecting it upon "reality." The real God has given us the free will that allows us to create such a graven image, but that image will never affect the real God.

Because God is formless, there are no conditions in the world of form that can have any effect whatsoever on God. No mental image that my human self or the false teachers have created will have the slightest effect on the reality of God. This more than anything else helped me see the difference between God's reality and the many, many mental images created by the forces of this world.

If I let myself believe in a man-made image it will *not* change reality, but it *will* change how I look at life, my life experience. Believing in a "graven image" is what causes me to reject God's unconditional love. The Danish state church had given me the impression that God would love me only if I lived up to certain conditions defined by this religion, such as not being a sinner. Of course, it also said I was a sinner by my very nature, so there seemed to be no way to receive God's love in this world.

Any image of God based on the forms we see in this world will inevitably define conditions that make me think God's love is conditional. But in seeking to earn the conditional love of a false God, I reject the unconditional love that the real God is offering me constantly. As long as we have not experienced unconditionality, we might think it is just a concept and thus the intellect can understand, analyze and categorize it as true or false. We might think we can use the linear, reasoning mind to come up with arguments for or against unconditional love.

After I experienced unconditionality, I knew it is completely beyond what the intellect is capable of handling.

What blocks unconditional love

Consider the question: "Which part of UNconditional don't you understand?" This is a koan, a riddle. The word *part* is a teaser because that which is unconditional can have no parts. Parts are separate entities, divisions, and they are set apart by conditions. The intellect is an analytical faculty; it is based on identifying differences and then using them to fit everything into a category in its database. Unconditionality cannot be divided into parts, and thus the intellect simply cannot deal with it.

That means, in essence, that we cannot "understand" unconditionality. We can know it *only* through direct experience. Of course, the intellect can create a concept of unconditionality, but in creating a concept, we have lost the real thing. We need a concept only when we do not have the direct experience.

Let's go to a deeper level. What is the illusion of separation really saying when it comes to God's love? It is saying that God's love is not found in this world and that we must enter paradise in order to receive God's love. What does this really mean? It means that somehow something has shut out God's love from this world. That "something" must be created in the world of form. How could something that has form, and thus is based on conditions, have the power to shut out a love that is unconditional? How can anything that has conditions ever have power over that which is UNconditional and which is therefore beyond the reach of conditions?

The illusion is also saying that in order to receive God's love, we have to enter paradise—we have to live up to certain conditions. What sense does it make that we have to live up to certain conditions in order to receive a love that is unconditional?

We have now reached a dividing line. If you have experienced some form of unconditionality, what I said in the preceding paragraphs will either seem self-evident to you or at least seem logical and worth further contemplation. If you have not experienced the unconditional or if you have not acknowledged the experience, what I said will seem like simply another concept and your intellect might already have come up with arguments against it.

This brings us to a profound truth: In order to receive God's unconditional love, we *only* have to accept it. Once we do accept it, we *will* begin to experience it. And once we do experience it, *everything* in our lives will begin to change.

That means that people who deny or argue against unconditional love simply cannot have experienced it. Why have they not experienced it? Well, how can we experience something that we deny and argue against? We cannot deny something and at the same time open ourselves up to experiencing oneness, gnosis, with it.

How do we experience the unconditional? It is the natural state of the pure self. The human self is created through an effort, a tension, and it is this tension that obscures unconditionality. So the simple way to experience the unconditional is to somehow get beyond the tension.

The problem is that many people do not want to get beyond the tension because they think they need the human self. The human self will literally tell us that if we go beyond the struggle, we will die. If we believe this, how can we ever open our minds to the unconditional? We can be reborn into a new sense of self only by being wiling to let the old sense of self die.

I am not trying to say that it is wrong to hold on to the human self or that people should agree with me. God has given us all free will. As a result, we decided that we wanted to experience what it was like to see ourselves as separate beings. If you have not had enough of that experience, who am I to tell you any different?

If what I have said makes any sense to you, it just might be because you too have tired of separation and you are now ready to come into oneness. I can tell you that oneness must be based on unconditionality because conditions can only divide us. Unconditional love is the key to true oneness. There can be no oneness if love is conditional.

I accepted God's unconditional love because I had experienced the formless Presence of God and I could not pin any man-made conditions on that experience. If you have not had that experience, what I say may seem like just another argument. However, I am convinced that people who sincerely apply themselves to the spiritual path will eventually have cleared their subconscious minds of so much baggage that the sun of unconditional love will start shining through the clouds. My experience has shown me that experiencing unconditional love is our natural state and it is unnatural to have it blocked by man-made conditions. Remove enough blocks and you return to your natural state. After all, the sun is always shining above the clouds. A consistent theme in this book has been that we need to identify how our minds have been programmed and then we need to transcend that programming. That is what just about every spiritual teacher has said. Jesus told his disciples to "leave your nets" and to "let the dead bury their dead." The Buddha told us to let go of attachments. In one of the original Star Wars movies, there is a situation where Luke Skywalker is being trained by the Jedi master, Yoda. His immortal remark is: "Luke, you must unlearn what you have learned." If we want to attain self-mastery, we must unlearn everything we have "learned" through the human self.

Growth-oriented versus feel-good spirituality

Let me point to another form of subtle programming. If you, like me, grew up watching American crime shows on television, you will have been programmed with a very simplistic view of life. There is a clearly defined problem. Someone is responsible for creating the problem. By bringing them to justice (or killing them), we solve the problem. And by the way, this can all be done in less than an hour.

If we apply this to the problem of self-esteem, we get the following scenario. The problem is that you don't have self-esteem. The reason is that something outside yourself has taken it or is not giving it to you. If you can change that something outside yourself, you will solve the problem. And this should happen in almost no time at all.

I grew up in Europe and lived in the United States for 22 years. I think I can allow myself to say that in my experience, many Americans are very impatient. Sometimes it seems as if delaying someone for one second in traffic is the greatest sin you could commit in today's America. I believe this ties in with what I like to call the "push-button mentality." It's an unrecognized mentality that basically says: "If it can't be done in five minutes, it ain't worth doing." That mentality has created a new "religion" based on the idea that for every problem there has to be a shortcut.

If we compare that to all of the spiritual and mystical traditions of the world, we will see that there are two divisions: the path of shortcuts and the path of long-term growth. Some spiritual books and teachers will indeed promise us that they have a shortcut. For example, they say that by making a few simple adjustments to our attitude, we will instantly improve our self-esteem. The question is, how long will this last when we are exposed to the pressures of everyday life? How many people come back from weekend courses with a positive attitude, only to have it evaporate during their first day at work?

I am not denying that changing our attitude works. We can quickly change our basic attitude to life and it can have almost instantaneous benefits. However, the human self is made from imperfect beliefs and misqualified energies and this self has been created over many lifetimes. Feel-good spirituality may make you feel good for a time, but as with any artificial stimulant, every high will be followed by a low.

What I have attempted to show you in this book is that there is a viable path to true self-esteem, but it is not a shortcut. It may produce some instant results, but it will take a sustained effort to receive the full results. If you follow the path I have described, you will get profound results that will have a lasting impact on your life.

Again, let's look at the "problem" of self-esteem. Why don't you have it? Because you are looking at yourself through the perception filter of your human self and this self will never attain lasting self-esteem. It will seek to build self-esteem by living up to a relative standard in this world. This can indeed give you a sense of self-esteem and many people have spent lifetimes pursuing this goal. But if it had worked, why would you be reading a book on the spiritual road to self-esteem?

The real way to solve the "problem" of self-esteem is to realize that there is no problem. The problem is not a real problem but a perceived problem that seems real only when we view it through the human self. The key to true self-esteem is to rise above the self that thinks it needs esteem from somewhere outside itself.

Theoretically, it is possible that you could instantly see this and then shift out of the human self. In my experience, most of us aren't able to go through such an instant awakening. Instead, we need to follow a gradual path of resolving both the energies and the limiting beliefs that keep us tied to the human self. Such a sustained effort is exactly what many spiritual teachers advocate. I call this growth-oriented spirituality as opposed to feel-good spirituality.

Making peace with the process

Right now each of us is facing a particular outer situation and a particular inner situation. The question is how you can move from where you are now to where you want to be? You may have specific problems you would like to overcome, such as low self-esteem. Behind any of these identifiable problems, where do you really want to go in life? What is the ultimate goal you would like to attain? What is the highest purpose you can see for your life?

Let me present you with a realization that I came to after many years and that I wish I had understood much earlier. When I was younger, I thought the goal of my life was to attain a higher state of consciousness and that is why I dedicated my life to the spiritual path.

The result was that for the first 25 years I was on the path, I was like a runner, running at full speed with my tongue hanging out, never having time to stop and smell the roses. I pursued spiritual growth with such ferocious determination that I had no attention left over for enjoying the journey. After all, the point of the journey was to get to the destination—wasn't it?

Well, yes and no. Today I see that my entire life is one long path and while there is an ultimate destination, it is still very far away. My motivation for walking the spiritual path is no longer to reach some ultimate state of consciousness here on earth. I am still pursuing a higher state of consciousness, but I now see that I will keep transcending my state of consciousness for as long as I am on this planet (and even beyond that).

I am no longer running, with my tongue sticking out, after some goal that always seems to be ahead of me. I have shifted from being focused on the result to being focused on the process itself. I can now enjoy the process instead of feeling like I will be suffering until I reach my final destination. Every time I take a step up in consciousness, I feel a sense of accomplishment and victory. I am at peace with being where I am on my path and knowing that while I will always be on my way, I can nevertheless enjoy every step of the journey.

What did it take for me to get to that point? Can telling you this help you make that shift instantly? Today I see that while my first 25 years on the path were not very enjoyable, it was a necessary phase I had to go through. I hope that by describing my journey, you can get through this phase in less time than it took me. What I was doing during most of those 25 years was not actually running towards a higher state of consciousness. Instead, I was running away from a lower state of consciousness. I was seeking to run away from one aspect of my human self, but in doing so I was running towards the opposite aspect.

During this phase, I had a lot of baggage I was dragging along. As I've explained, this baggage was made up of the limiting beliefs of my human self (which I believed were true or which I had never questioned) and the energies that I had misqualified through those beliefs. The result was that my mind was a turbulent place in which I could find no peace. I was trying to run away from this inner turmoil, and the turmoil prevented me from enjoying the journey, driving me to run faster and faster.

The basic dynamic of this phase was that I was focused on a result and I felt I could not be at peace until I had attained the result. Today I am no longer focused on a result, but I am at peace with the process. Does that mean my result-focus was wrong? Not at all.

It was a very necessary phase of my path. However, if I had known what I know today, I think I could have shortened that period and more quickly come to the point where I could be at peace with and enjoy my personal path. I am hoping I can help you make peace with being on the present stage of your personal path while still doing what helps you move towards the next stage.

Instant awakening or a systematic path?

I have come across a few spiritual teachers who claim to be enlightened. They also claim that their enlightenment happened spontaneously, meaning that they did not follow a systematic path that led them (mechanically or automatically) to enlightenment. Some of them even deny the validity of following such a path and say that the more you focus on following a path, the more you will block enlightenment. I agree with that, but only up to a point.

I agree that the path to a higher state of consciousness is not a mechanical or automatic path. I agree that many people, myself included, have approached the spiritual path through the filter of the human self. We therefore use the perception filter of the human self to define a goal for the spiritual path and the steps we need to take in order to get there.

That can cause us to define a false or outer path, and the more vigorously we pursue it, the more we will actually reinforce the human self and thus block our enlightenment—the point where we snap out of identifying with the human self. However, I also see that we simply cannot do anything else. When we find the spiritual path, we are in a certain state of consciousness and we can only approach the path through the filter of that state of mind.

Where I stop agreeing with such teachers is where they say that enlightenment can only happen spontaneously so we don't need to do anything to attain it. What such teachers are essentially saying is: "I attained enlightenment spontaneously, and all you have to do is have a spontaneous awakening like me. And by the way, if you can't have that, you are simply not advanced enough. Sorry, come back in your next lifetime."

When I was going through my turbulent phase, what good would it have done me to have a teacher say: "Oh, just stop all your efforts, sit down on your rear end and wait for spontaneous awakening." If I had followed such advice, I am pretty sure I would still be sitting there waiting for spontaneous awakening, and I might end up sitting there for lifetimes. Furthermore, I would have stayed in my state of inner turmoil until the moment I had my spontaneous awakening.

Based on my own experience, I believe that there is a process of spiritual growth. There is, in a sense, a mechanical aspect to spiritual growth in that we have accumulated a certain amount of lower energies in the four levels of our minds. This energy creates our inner turmoil because our minds are like a boiling pot. The first phase of the spiritual path is to seek to reduce the inner turmoil. Obviously, this can be done in many ways and I am not claiming there is only one way that works. For myself, I have found nothing more effective than using the decrees and invocations given by the ascended masters to invoke spiritual light.

Using such techniques will help reduce our inner turmoil, but the techniques themselves cannot take us to a higher state of consciousness. That is because after the turmoil is reduced, we need to look at the mechanism that caused us to generate the lower energies in the first place. That mechanism is that in the past, including in past lives, we were exposed to traumatic situations and we reacted to them by creating or adopting certain beliefs. These beliefs form the elements of our human selves, and the only way to become free of them is to consciously see a belief and then replace it with a higher realization. This can never be a mechanical process. It is more like a creative process because it requires us to make conscious decisions.

I spent several years invoking light and reducing my inner turmoil to the point where I was ready to go into therapy and look at some of my more obvious psychological hang-ups. As a result of going into therapy, combined with my studies of spiritual teachings and popular psychology, I experienced that I could indeed overcome the baggage from my past. I believe that anyone applying a similar approach can achieve the same results.

We live in a very fortunate time because we have both spiritual teachings and psychological healing methods that can help us turn our lives into an upward spiral. An upward spiral means that we have reduced the inner turmoil to a manageable level and we have learned how to identify and leave behind limiting beliefs. Once you have overcome a certain amount of emotional pain and limiting beliefs, you realize that the spiritual path works and you begin to see that there really is no limit to how far it can take you. I can tell you this, but it won't impact your life until you experience it yourself. The proof of the pudding is in the eating.

The decision to accept yourself

Anyone who applies themselves to the spiritual path can get to the point where they have started an upward spiral. Once you are at that point, you have the opportunity to make a conscious decision. I did not make that decision as early as I might have for the simple reason that I was trapped in the mindset that my goal was a higher state of consciousness and thus I could not allow myself to enjoy life or feel at peace until I got there. In effect, I felt that until I reached this superhuman state of consciousness, I would not have ultimate self-esteem. Today I know this was an immature approach that prolonged my lack of peace for several years and it was unnecessary. When we come to the point of knowing that we can transcend the past, we have the opportunity to stop and take stock of our path. We can then acknowledge that we are sincere spiritual seekers. We are not engaged in illegal or immoral activities and we would never deliberately hurt anyone. We have sincerely studied spiritual teachings and we have diligently applied spiritual tools. We have been willing to look at ourselves in the mirror and work on our psychological hang-ups. We have indeed made progress on the path towards transcending the human self and all of its contradictions and we are committed to continuing this progress.

At this point, we can then accept that this is all that God and our spiritual teachers require of us. The ascended masters have taught me that they do not take a quick-fix approach to helping us grow. They look at the long-term perspective and they see that our growth in consciousness will continue as long as we are on earth and even beyond that in the spiritual realm. The masters see that we will not attain the ultimate state of consciousness until we achieve full God awareness, and that will not happen for a very long time. Thus, the masters know that for an almost indefinite future, we will be on the path of moving towards a goal without being there yet. As a result of this, the ascended masters have no desire whatsoever for us to feel inadequate or feel that we cannot have self-esteem until we reach a superhuman state of consciousness.

The simple fact is that you can attain a healthy sense of self-esteem long before you reach a superhuman state of consciousness. The only way to attain this state of self-esteem is to shift your sense of self away from a deficit approach. If you keep focusing on the glass being half-empty and beating yourself up over not yet having attained cosmic consciousness, you will remain trapped in the human self. As I said, the worthy part of the human self will forever keep pounding on you that you are not worthy until you achieve some ultimate state of spiritual growth. It will use whatever spiritual teaching you follow to create a new standard for you, a standard that you can never actually meet. The unworthy self will pound on you that you are not worthy no matter what you do. Both the worthy and the unworthy self are saying that you are not worthy—yet.

You can learn to recognize that this is simply a control mechanism employed by your human self. You can then make a conscious decision that you will no longer allow your human self to pull you around like a bull with a ring through its nose. All that really stands in your way is to dismiss the self-image that you are an unworthy being striving towards perfection. Instead, consider that God created you as a being who is constantly striving to transcend your current sense of self. You are not created just to achieve a final result. You are created as a process-oriented being and you have the right to allow yourself to enjoy the process of growing towards a higher state. Rather than focusing on how far you still have to go, allow yourself to feel that each forward step gives you the fullness of victory.

You will never achieve true self-esteem as the result of a mechanical process. There is nothing you can do that will one day produce a big "PUFF" and then you have perfect self-esteem. Achieving true self-esteem is a result of you making a conscious decision to accept that you are worthy in your present state of becoming. I know very well that you may still have so much inner turmoil or so many unresolved human beliefs that you cannot apply my words right now. Yet there is a viable path you can follow.

I also know that there are millions of people who have been following the spiritual path to the best of their ability for years or even decades. Many of these people are indeed at the point where they could make the shift in consciousness and come to accept themselves as being fully worthy spiritual students who are on the upward path.

When I look back at my 36 years on the spiritual path, I am amazed at how much more I understand today and how many psychological limitations I have overcome. I still have things come up in my psychology that I have not resolved. I used to think: "How much more unresolved psychology can there be?" Today I know there will be unresolved stuff to overcome for as long as I am here on this planet, and I am at peace with that. I no longer beat myself up for not being perfect. I am at peace with being a sincere student who is on the path and who is willing to look at anything that comes to my attention and work on transcending it. And that is a very good place to be.

If you ask me whether I am enlightened, I would have no answer for you. Partly because I have simply lost interest in evaluating myself based on a standard with some predefined goal or comparing myself to others. My only goal is constant self-transcendence and I see this as a lifelong process.

Enlightenment cannot be defined. The process of awakening is the process of transcending the perception filters of the human self. The human self thinks it can define everything, including what it means to be enlightened. If you think you have a definition of what it means to be enlightened or awakened and you use it to make declarations about yourself, aren't you demonstrating that you are not there yet? I used to think that enlightenment meant that you had achieved some ultimate state of consciousness from which no more progress was possible.

Now I see that enlightenment is an ongoing process and it really is meaningless to divide it into these separate compartments. I am content to be more enlightened today than I was yesterday and I am determined to be more enlightened tomorrow than I am today.

When I was 20 years old, someone told me that he saw me as a person who was "definitely on your way." My reaction was "On my way to what?" I am still on my way, but the difference is that today I am happy being on my way without having an absolute goal in the foreseeable future. It's both empowering and liberating when your self-esteem comes from the process rather than the result. And it is far better to be on the way than to be in your own way.

Keys from Chapter 8

◊   You cannot achieve **ultimate self-esteem** without knowing the self, and you cannot know the self without dealing with your personal relationship to God. The reason for that is that the pure self is an extension of God's Being.

◊   **God is beyond all form** and thus God loves you with a love that is beyond conditions. It is a great challenge to accept this unconditional love from God, but it is the ultimate key to healing.

◊   **The human self will always reject** unconditional love and will seek to define conditions that you need to meet in order to receive God's love. The only condition you need to meet in order to receive unconditional love is that you accept it without conditions.

◊   **Your human self and intellect** cannot understand the unconditional, but you can experience it when the pure self steps outside the human perception filter.

◊   There comes a point on your personal path when the only thing holding you back is that you must make a conscious decision to **accept yourself as worthy of God's love.**

EPILOGUE

The vast majority of spiritual people I meet have a clear sense that they are here at this time in order to help make the earth a better place—to help society make a quantum leap towards a more spiritual approach to life. Since the 1960s, millions of people in the Western world have experimented with spiritual teachings. While we have had a positive impact on society, I believe this impact has not been as powerful or as pervasive as it could have been. What might be blocking the impact we could be having?

I have already mentioned that in Denmark there is a growing awareness that the biggest challenge for public health care will be mental health. We can see the same tendency in all industrialized countries. More and more people suffer from mental illness and more and more people run into social problems, crime and substance abuse. After the financial crisis of 2008, unemployment has skyrocketed among young people and there is talk about a "lost generation" who have no prospects of getting a job and who consequently see no purpose for their lives.

It doesn't take much to see that Western society is heading for a crisis. In my view, it is not an economic, social or political crises—it is a spiritual crisis. Of course, society doesn't see it that way. But why not? Because those of us who are spiritual have not been able to get our message across. I think this is slowly changing and that we are facing a golden opportunity.

A natural phase in human evolution

I believe that what the Western world is going through is not actually a crisis but simply the next logical step in our growth as a civilization. My great grandfather lived in the late 1800s and early 1900s. He had 13 children and worked 12 hours a day, six days a week in a dirty, noisy factory job. His life was clearly focused on fighting to provide the material necessities for his family, and things like spiritual growth or resolving his psychology were not even on his radar screen. My grandfather also worked factory jobs his entire life, and during the 1930s and during the Nazi occupation of Denmark it was still a struggle to stay out of poverty.

My parents were also working-class people, but during the 1960s they started having a materially secure lifestyle. Of course, I have grown up in a time where many people have actually had the incredible luxury of being able to provide for their material needs while having time, energy and money left over for other activities as well. This explains why millions of people have been able to pursue their spiritual goals over the past several decades.

When you look at this development, you can see that for most of the past century our Western societies have been focused on providing the material conditions that could lift people out of poverty. There is nothing wrong with this and it was a perfectly necessary and natural phase in our growth as a civilization. What our society has not done is stop and ask some questions about what comes next. Is a modern affluent society really a goal in itself, or is it merely a phase towards an even higher goal?

What might be the next logical step for modern civilization? When I was young, I used to feel that it was wrong, and primitive, that I had grown up in a society that could not provide its young people with a real sense that their lives have a purpose and that what they do matters in a larger context. I used to blame this on mainstream Christianity and its talk about sinners and on scientific materialism and its claim that we are little more than hairless apes.

Today I don't blame this on anyone but see it as an inevitable consequence of our history. I also see that unless we clarify our vision of the next step for civilization, we will indeed end up in a crisis that could become as turbulent as what we are right now seeing in several Arab countries. The old ways must give way for the next step, and the more a society holds on to the old, the more turmoil it will take for that society to break free of the past.

A new resource for society

What can avoid a crisis and give modern civilization a more smooth transition to the next level? My vision is that we absolutely need to transcend the focus on materialism. As just one aspect of this, we need to give people, especially young people, a real sense of purpose. To me, neither Christianity nor materialism can do this as has already been proven. The only thing that has a chance of accomplishing this goal is spirituality— but not just any form of spirituality. In my view, we need to develop a universal approach to spirituality.

When I look back at my own experience with spiritual movements, I see a very clear tendency. Most of us grew up in a society that had no answers to our spiritual questions and we then found a philosophy, guru or organization that gave us such answers. It is therefore natural that we sometimes come to believe that if only we can convert the rest of the world to follow our specific teaching, we will be able to solve society's problems. I let go of this belief a long time ago and I believe millions of other people have done the same. It simply isn't realistic that the rest of the world will be converted to follow one specific spiritual teacher or teaching.

I do believe it is possible to get many people in the Western world to adopt a more universal approach to spirituality. I am not going to try to define this approach here, but I do feel it will be focused on our growth in consciousness, our potential to escape the human state of consciousness and reach a higher state in which we can exercise the fullness of our creative potential.

When you accept that you have the potential to rise above human misery and reach a higher state of consciousness, your life instantly takes on a profound sense of meaning and purpose. You realize that your real career is your growth in consciousness—not to work in some job for 40 years and retire with a gold watch. If society could accept such a universal view, we could see that the primary goal of modern society is actually to provide the material conditions that allow the greatest number of people to pursue a growth in consciousness.

This could bring many profound changes. For example, I have always felt it is amazing that our society teaches children about technological devices but does not teach them how to operate the device that affects everything they do in life, namely their own psyches. Why shouldn't we bring up children from an early age to be aware of how the human psyche works and that they have the potential to master their own reactions and rise above their psychological limitations?

Is it really so bad if young people spend several years being unemployed? As long as society helps them meet minimum material needs, isn't it a wonderful opportunity for them to focus on raising their consciousness? Wouldn't it be far better that they seek to improve themselves than spend their time drinking, taking drugs or getting into gangs and crime?

Why wouldn't society see it as an important resource that people seek to raise their consciousness and thereby unlock the creativity that might, at some point in their lives, help them bring forth ideas that could contribute to solving some of society's problems? Why wouldn't business see this as another resource, especially since many businesses are already using various tools that are psycho-spiritual in nature?

While space might be the final frontier, the mind is the ultimate frontier. We might run out of certain physical resources, but we will be in real trouble only if we run out of creativity. Raising your consciousness through a deliberate and systematic process is the ultimate way to unlock creativity and thus it is the ultimate resource for a civilization that has reached the point of being able to provide for our material needs. It would be a waste to ignore this potential while complaining that we are running out of resources and solutions.

A unique opportunity for spiritual people

How can the equation change? If society is going to adopt a universal spiritual approach, how might this come about? It can come about only through people, and who might give such an impetus to society if not the people who have already experimented with the process of raising their consciousness?

Western society is on the brink of unlocking the potential of the mind and taking a quantum leap into a new era of creative solutions. I believe we who are the spiritual people are meant to be the forerunners of this shift. Many have already started doing this by expressing their spirituality in their daily lives and work situations, but many more need to jump on the bandwagon.

What will it take for you to make a shift so that you can feel free to see your spiritual experience as a valid resource and express it? First, I think it's necessary to overcome the belief that the spiritual revolution will happen by everyone becoming the followers of one spiritual teacher or teaching. Second, I encourage you to accept that because you are a sincere spiritual student and have gained experience with transcending your state of consciousness, you do have something to offer to other people and to society.

I even foresee that in coming decades there will be job opportunities for those who have experience with the basic process of self-transcendence and who can help others do the same. Today we have an establishment of psychologists and social counselors who could be much more effective if they had a more spiritual outlook. Prescribing people drugs that dull their minds is a poor substitute for helping people master their minds. Another example is the religious field.

In Denmark, for example, there is a state church funded by taxpayer money. However, the vast majority of the taxpayers never go to church. The reason is that the priests are not able to meet people's psycho-spiritual needs. This means that the state is funding the physical churches and paying the pastors for a service that helps a shrinking number of people. At the same time, people are increasingly seeking help with psycho-spiritual problems from the healthcare system.

This simply isn't sustainable and one alternative would be to create a position for people who have experience with both spirituality and psychology. Some educational systems already seek to unite the two, but much more could be done if society made it a priority to create paid positions for professionals who could help people with their psycho-spiritual needs based on both education *and* personal experience. There are already people who have this experience; it is only a matter of seeing this as a resource and making use of it.

I believe the shift has already begun, but it needs to be accelerated greatly in order to make a real difference in society. Who can help accomplish this? Only the millions of people who have personal experience with spiritual growth and who have reached a level of real self-esteem based on knowledge of their true self. I hope that if this book has helped you claim a higher level of self-esteem, you will consider how you can use your spiritual background to help other people and help take society to its logical next step. After all, the natural consequence of acquiring true self-esteem is that you use it to help other people and help raise the whole of which you now know you are a part. I believe every sincere spiritual student has a valuable contribution to make and I hope this book helps you find yours.

ACKNOWLEDGEMENTS

I am deeply grateful for the efforts of Nigel J. Yorwerth and Patricia Spadaro of PublishingCoaches.com in helping us with the development and packaging of this book through its many stages. I am indebted to them both for their expert advice and guidance.

I offer my heartfelt thanks and gratitude to my wife, Helen, who stood by me and supported me through the process of giving birth to this book by cheering me on and giving me valuable feedback as the manuscript was taking shape. I am grateful to friends and acquaintances I have met along life's way for sharing with me your presence and stories that illumined the lessons in this book.

Kim Michaels is an accomplished writer and author. He has conducted spiritual conferences and workshops in 14 countries and has counseled hundreds of spiritual students. He is also cohost of the weekly radio show Divine Love Talk. For more information, visit Kim at www.KimMichaels.info and www.transcendencetoolbox.com.